THE UNPROMISED LAND

The Struggle of Messianic Jews

GARY & SHIRLEY
BERESFORD

THE UNPROMISED LAND

THE STRUGGLE OF MESSIANIC JEWS

GARY & SHIRLEY BERESFORD

BY LINDA ALEXANDER

LEDERER MESSIANIC PUBLICATIONS
Baltimore, Maryland

DEDICATION

This book is dedicated first and foremost to *HaShem* (the Lord), who has equipped us for the struggle; then to our parents and those of our people who never lost the vision for the right of the Jewish people to live in the land of Israel according to the promises of the God of Israel; and, finally, to all who have been involved in the writing and publishing of this chronicle.

> *Arise, shine, for your light has come, and the glory of the Lord has risen upon you.*
>
> — Isaiah 60:1

6204 Park Heights Avenue, Baltimore, MD 21215, U.S.A.

ISBN 1-800226-56-1
Printed in the United States of America
Cover & Book Design by Steffi Rubin

CONTENTS

FOREWORD

"Some are born great, others achieve greatness, and others have greatness thrust upon them." It is the third part of Shakespeare's epigram that applies to Gary and Shirley Beresford. They were born into circumstances well within the range of ordinary; and their achievements, while respectable, would not normally evoke the accolades that pertain to greatness. But circumstances during the last seven and one half years have called forth from within these simple and ordinary people the strength and the steadfast pursuit of a righteous purpose that deserves the name "greatness."

And what have these people, these friends of mine whom I call "simple" and "ordinary" done? Like millions of Jews before them, including myself, they have tried to make *aliyah*—immigrate to Israel—under the Law of Return, which gives any Jew, anywhere in the world the right to become a citizen of Israel and live here. But unlike the other millions, they have been refused. Not only were they refused, but twice Israel's High Court of Justice declared them ineligible on the ground that they had become "members of another religion" and therefore not "Jews" for the purposes of the Law of Return. And the reason is simply because they believe that the Messiah of Israel has already come once and is coming again as promised in the *Tanakh*—the Hebrew Scriptures, or "Old Testament"—and that the name of this Messiah is Yeshua—Jesus. In its 1989 decision the Court determined that Messianic Jews (Jews who accept Yeshua as Israel's Messiah) are the one group of born Jews who may not immigrate to Israel under the Law of Return—they are Israel's only *refusniks.*

The Beresfords have been at the focus and the cutting edge of these developments—not because they sought a battle, but because they, like the millions, sought to live in the land promised to their forefathers Abraham, Isaac and Jacob. They have withstood pressure from family, from friends, from Christians, from Jews, even from other Messianic Jews, urging them to give up and slink away. But they have not done so. Yeshua has given them the strength and determination to pursue their goal. They are, this day, living in the land of Israel, continuing to inquire after such options as remain open to them. And those of us who support them and their cause, who believe that Messianic Jews should be allowed, like all other Jews, to make *aliyah* under the Law of Return, appreciate their steadfastness. We see how our Messiah has worked in their lives, bringing them to a maturity of faith that deserves emulation.

Therefore I am honored to have been asked to write the foreword to their story. And I pray—and covet your prayers—that they and all Messianic Jews will soon be permitted by the State of Israel to make *aliyah* as Jews under the Law of Return and to live, like millions of other Jews, with neither fear nor persecution in the Promised Land.

David H. Stern
Chairman, Committee for the Three Families
Translator, *Jewish New Testament*
Author, *Jewish New Testament Commentary*
Messianic Jewish Manifesto
Restoring the Jewishness of the Gospel

Jerusalem
May 1, 1994

Chapter One
PROLOGUE

"How, Gary? How could the South African Zionist Federation *and* the Ministry of the Interior of Israel learn of our belief in Yeshua as Messiah?" Shirley shook her head. She looked at her husband, the question hanging between them. "I need to know exactly how this happened."

She sat with Gary in the living room of their Israeli home, wrestling over and over with the facts. A letter from the Ministry of the Interior sat before them. The cold letter bluntly stated that they had been denied citizenship by the government of Israel. The letterhead at the top of the official document read: Ministry of the Interior. The denial of their request was based on their beliefs in Yeshua as the Messiah.

Neither Shirley nor Gary could understand why their personal beliefs were being used to deny them a citizenship. After all, citizenship was their right! A right virtually ensured by a 1950 governmental edict allowing—no, *inviting*—anyone of Jewish matriarchal heritage to immigrate to Israel.

Gary and Shirley continued to read together through the letter and attached papers. They stated that there was sufficient "evidence" to prove that they had converted to another religion.

Converted! The word stood there as an accusation.

The Law of Return granted immigration only to prospective immigrants who had not converted from Judaism. The Beresfords, the letter stated, did not fit the criteria. They had clearly, in the official eyes of the Ministry, changed their religion. Hence, they were no longer Jews.

"Don't fit the criteria?" Gary asked no one in particular. His voice was incredulous. "Why, we've become even *more* Jewish since we accepted Yeshua. How can they say we are no longer Jews?!"

Shirley put her hand in his. She had no words of comfort as she shared her husband's exasperation. The court had examined the evidence and had found conclusively, without any doubt, that the Beresfords were simply unacceptable.

Suddenly, Shirley became rigid and her hands shook. "Oh no!," she cried, continuing to read. Each line made her eyes widen more. Her entire body began to quiver. "No! No, no, no." She rocked back and forth. Tears flowed down her flushed face and on to her neck.

The court wrote that Shirley's own son, Javin, from her previous marriage, had "turned them in." Speaking to the South African Zionist Federation months earlier, Javin's testimony caused his parent's first request for citizenship to be denied. His words had triggered the sequence of events which would continue to haunt them to this day.

Tragic and ironic that, of all Shirley's six children, Javin had been the one to do such a traitorous thing. A few years earlier, while visiting them in Harare, Zimbabwe, Javin had accepted

Yeshua as Messiah. Returned to Johannesburg, he began attending a Bible believing church. He had even been baptized in the name of Jesus.

He, too, had believed in Yeshua. Why would he betray his parents for the same belief? It was Gary who remembered the events that had caused Javin's change of heart.

"It was the Hasidim, love," Gary prompted, softly. "Remember?"

Shirley slowly nodded, wiping away her tears. She knew, with all her being, that the Lubavitch Hasidim had to be behind her son's tragic turnaround. The Beresfords had learned of Javin's involvement with the ultra-Orthodox group shortly after the couple had first applied for Israeli citizenship.

The Lubavitch Hasidim were an extreme Jewish sect committed to converting Jews to their specific brand of Orthodoxy. Their ways and views differed greatly from those of mainstream Judaism and their ideology was restricted to a relatively small segment—perhaps one or two per cent of the worlds's 15,000,000 Jews. Nonetheless, they were zealous, aggressive, and extremely persuasive to those who heard and accepted their fervent message.

Retracing the chain of events, Gary and Shirley remembered how Javin had come to them during one of their recent visits to Zimbabwe. A storm gathered over his handsome face and he was full of fury and uncontrollable rage.

"You have become a Christian," Javin had spat out accusingly at his mother. "A Christian!" His words were spoken as if they were a curse, something dirty.

The accusation had come as a surprise. Hadn't Javin understood when he himself had put his faith in Yeshua? Shirley looked at her son. Apparently he did not understand. Centuries of historical confusion once again clouded the issue of a Jewish person believing in the Jewish Messiah. Once again the issue became a question of misunderstood labels and names that had strayed far from their original meanings.

Shirley stared at her son, not knowing what to say, how to

explain, where to begin to untangle the confusion. Now she realized that, to Javin's way of thinking, she and Gary had turned their backs on their Jewishness when they had embraced Yeshua. His opinion of their new belief was clear. Javin had done the only thing he could think of to force his mother to abandon her "misguided" faith.

Now here they were, staring at the results. Gary and Shirley were certain that Javin had been influenced by the Lubavitch Hasidim to stand against them and their decision to immigrate to Israel. As a Jewish son, it was his responsibility to report even his parents if they accepted a belief foreign to traditional Judaism. He thought he had done what was best for them and what was best for him, as well as what would benefit all Jews. A Jew who believed in Yeshua as the Messiah could never be accepted, not even by the closest of family members.

Although Gary and Shirley had been disturbed when they had first learned of Javin's involvement with a Hasidic family, never did they imagine that her son would follow his fears this far. This single action by Shirley's flesh and blood, one of her own children, had erected the roadblock which now barred Gary and Shirley from accomplishing one of their life's dreams—to live in the land that God had promised to the Jews.

"How could he do this to us?" Gary bellowed, bursting out of his seat, pacing the floor. He walked the length of the room, and then turned and stomped back. "How could he do it to *you*, his own mother?" Gary's hands were balled into fists, his color was rising.

Shirley looked helplessly up at him. Her expression offered no answer, no justification for her son's betrayal. Unable to stop the flow of her tears, she convulsed with sobs. Words wouldn't leave her mouth. She could only shake her head, over and over. Gary's anger swelled again.

"I feel like ripping him apart!"

Then Gary dropped back into his seat, cradling his wife in his arms. He was unable to bear what misery this discovery might begin in her. It could quite possibly completely undo her newly-found sense of well-being. Her recovery from depression was still so fresh; only recently had she been strong enough to turn away from a debilitating dependence on medication. He was certain that something this devastating, this heartbreaking, could push her right back into that dark world.

It just wasn't fair that her life had to be put on the edge all over again. How on earth could this have happened to her? To them?

Chapter Two

SHIRLEY

Shirley's earliest years were spent in the untamed beauty of the South African countryside on the outskirts of Pretoria—dangerous, solitary, lonely. Her parents, who both lived and worked there, were forever concerned about raising their daughter in such an environment with only a housekeeper to watch her.

Hoping that Shirley would receive a solid education in a well-rounded social environment, they made the painful, difficult decision to place her in a Catholic convent boarding school. It was their honest belief that this would be best for her, insuring her safety and guarding her from the struggles found in the "real world."

The fact that they were Jewish didn't seem to concern them in their decision-making. The convent was by far the most structured, acceptable environment available to them. Religion didn't enter the picture.

A very young child, only six years old, Shirley observed and noted every crack in the gray, angry-looking buildings as she and her parents drove up the road to the convent. Certain that those blocks of ugly stone would soon come to represent something hateful in her life, she instinctively fought being there. She didn't want to be away from her mother and father. Lonely already, Shirley hadn't even moved in yet.

Her parents, however, had made up their minds and there was no room for argument. Little Shirley clung to her mother's skirts as the nuns forcefully peeled her away. Tears ran unchecked down her reddened cheeks as she stood shivering, surrounded by her cold, dark stone prison. Her parents had left her alone with these strange, unfriendly women.

Nothing was explained to her. Taken to what she was summarily told would be her dormitory, an unfriendly room shared by eight or so other little girls, Shirley cried uncontrollably for what seemed like hours. No attention was paid to her sorrow.

She lived in her own private world despite the other children constantly around her. The women, "nuns" they were called, wore plain black dresses that touched the floor. Their stern faces peeked ominously out of starched white and black hats. Shirley stayed out of their way as much as possible, but, when she had to be with them, just one of their brief glances would petrify her. The atmosphere was foreboding and the women were nothing like her mother. Shirley was crushed by a separation she didn't understand; no one seemed inclined to help sort out her confusion.

As the days wore on in the same monotonous routine, she convinced herself that her parents no longer loved her. Over and over she examined the evidence of her miserable life and could finally admit no other conclusion. They *couldn't* love her and still put her away in such a mean, hurtful place.

Yet she had no choice but to live there, to stay until she could find a way to be free. Only a child, she had to do as she was told. She had nowhere else to go. For now, this was her life. She must learn to adapt to this world which held no connection to the world she had always known.

It didn't take long for Shirley to feel in every part of her being how different she was from the others around her, both adults and children alike. She was Jewish, the nuns continually reminded her, an ugly, menacing tone in their voices. Because she was Jewish, she was forced to suffer ongoing punishment at the hands of the nuns. In her young face, they somehow saw the people who had killed their Lord, their Savior, Jesus Christ.

Often, Shirley was called "Christ killer."

Living in a Catholic convent, the strange, mysterious symbols and practices of Catholicism constantly bombarded her senses and pricked her curiosity. Yet, on the occasions when she saw her parents and asked them if she could go to mass like the other girls, they forbade her from entering the church.

And that cross, that "crucifix," as the nuns called it. It was present everywhere, hanging around every corner she turned, a constant reminder that, no matter how hard she tried, she could never be like those with whom she lived. Her parents had sent her away, and the people around her left her alone. Where was she to turn?

Despite the hurt, the loneliness, the confusion, Shirley was unable to quell the growing fascination she experienced concerning the man who was nailed to that cross. Bright red blood dripped from his wrists, ankles, forehead, mouth, and the nuns called him Jesus Christ; the one she was supposed to have killed.

But Shirley was only a scared, lonely little girl. She hadn't killed anyone, had she? How could she have? Despite her parents' orders that she never attend Mass, Shirley felt compelled one day to sneak into the church and sink to her knees. She was unable to stay away.

Something inside her told her she had to find out more about all this if she was ever to try and understand anything about life.

She heard the people around her unconsciously praying in the name of this man, this Jesus, whispering, almost chanting his name with reverence, as if they spoke of the King of England.

No, it was more than that. They worshipped this Jesus.

Sitting in the back, she bobbed her head from side to side to try and see over the heads in front of her. Slowly, almost fearfully, her eyes inched up until she was looking directly at the biggest cross she had seen yet. Her mouth fell open and she stared, unable to tear her eyes away.

It made no sense to her. W*hy* was the man there? How could *she* possibly be responsible for him being there? Why was he hanging like that on a cross, in full sight of all these people? Why did there have to be so many of these crosses everywhere she turned?

□□□

It seemed like a relief to Shirley when, at seventeen, after years of bouncing back and forth between the convent and various relatives, she married Julius Weinstein. He was a nice, friendly man whom she had met at a relative's wedding. Marriage would be the perfect way out, she decided. An opportunity to have a home of her own—a real, permanent home where she could garden and raise animals—and maybe children. Love? Well, love was something Shirley really didn't know much about. She would simply settle for less than love. At least, she believed, she would have peace.

Her first child, Lewis, was born a year later. As her marriage slid into a monotonous daily routine, the days went by in a blur. Her existence seemed to become more and more meaningless. Similar to life in the convent, the main difference was that now she didn't have to live with the nuns. Marriage to Julius harbored no revelations, no assurance that this was the life for which she'd been waiting. Somehow, the daily fears she had lived with for so many years had followed her. Without the convent or the nuns to blame for her malaise, Shirley began to worry.

And that man, that Jesus, seemed to follow her, too. Try as she might, she could not forget him. Her childlike impressions of awe remained in the recesses of her memory. Recollections would sometimes nag at her, as if they were trying to reveal something. The memories were so confused and they didn't fit into her new life. She would push them away, to the back of her thoughts, but she couldn't rid herself of them altogether.

After the birth of her third child, Steffan, Shirley finally made the difficult admission to herself that marriage had not provided the answer for which she'd been searching. Marriage itself did not give her true peace, nor could it offer a reason to continue living. She had escaped her original dreaded living arrangements, only to find herself trapped inside another prison of daily discontent.

What could she do about it? What were her options? She felt she had none. It became apparent, even to her, that she was giving in to debilitating fits of depression. At first this concerned her very much. She frantically made appointments with a variety of doctors.

She went looking for help, hoping for a simple fix, the right pill to make her life right itself. She began to suspect a new and fatal illness was behind her problems. Every stress, each ache, minor or major, affected her to the point of almost total incapacitation.

Doctor after doctor seemed to offer his own unique answer. Each one would add another pill to the growing regimen of Shirley's daily medication. Eventually she would be on eighteen pills a day. Without pills, she had come to believe she would be unable to function. With children to take care of, a house to run, a husband to emotionally support, functioning was not merely an option, it was a necessity.

The cycle of doctor visits continued, as did the medications. Shirley was eventually diagnosed as a manic-depressive, with no foreseeable chance for future rehabilitation. Life without medicine became unreal, unattainable. Strong tranquilizers, antidepressants, sleeping pills became accepted by Shirley and her family as the inevitable course for the rest of her life.

She lived in a state of perpetual drowsiness. Unaware of and unimpacted by the ups and downs of normal living, she became physically and emotionally detached. Paralyzing fear would come upon her as soon as the medication would begin to wear off. The drugs kept terror at bay.

Somewhere in the back of her consciousness, behind the prescription haze, Shirley vaguely understood that she wanted to break free from the horror that now inhabited her mind. She somehow realized that the traumas of her past had resulted in these stifling, and nagging, recurring feelings she was caught up in. A maelstrom of memories flooded her mind. The pressure of past experiences and present woes collided painfully inside her. She did not want to continue to live this way.

But she had no idea how to change things. She no longer had the strength to try. The more she sought a way out, the more depressed she became. Overpowering fear seemed to insidiously squeeze and choke each shaky breath out of her. She was petrified of absolutely everything.

Deep inside, Shirley was certain that the way out of this nightmare, if there was a way out, lay somewhere outside herself. There had to be some power far beyond anything she'd ever witnessed.

In an attempt to discover that elusive power, she threw herself into various spiritual pursuits, unhealthy relationships, psychotherapy—anything that offered a way out of her deep, personal pain. Her intense thirst for peace and freedom caused Shirley to drink deeply of each attempt at escape. All she wanted was some relief.

Not ready to abandon her cabinet of medications, Shirley added to her daily regimen other drug-like endeavors: Transcendental Meditation, yoga, chanting daily mantras. It became an obsession with her to seek out and try all religious activities. She even went so far as to attend a meeting where mediums called up dead souls in out-and-out occult worship.

Nothing worked. Instead, her experiments seemed to aggravate her frantic paranoia. Frustration became secondary only to her anguish. Shirley began to experience the sensation that everything—including time—was closing in on her, clawing at her. Soon she would lose total control of her life. The tenuous thread by which Shirley held on to reality was frayed and ready to snap.

Desperate, Shirley located an organization called Religious Science of the Mind International, and threw herself fully into the practice of "Positive Thinking." The group promised to teach her to focus only on the positive, to never allow anything negative to invade her being. In doing so, life would right itself. Everything would be okay.

It was another futile effort. Nothing ever seemed to be enough to satisfy Shirley's overwhelming need to find a true meaning and direction for her existence. Nothing was able to pull her out of her pool of fear.

Meanwhile, her husband, Julius, had made the hard decision that he could no longer deal with Shirley's depression and paranoia. It was destroying him as well as their life together.

Once they both admitted that there was no future for their marriage, Julius moved out and Shirley and the children stayed together, in their house. This arrangement worked for a year after the divorce, at which time Shirley learned that her father had a terminal illness. He had called Shirley and her ex-husband, Julius, to his bedside. As Shirley held her beloved father's hand, Julius stood silently behind her. Her father's whispery voice asked them, lovingly, heartbroken, to forget their divorce. Her father wanted them to make one more attempt to make a go of their marriage, for the sake of the children.

Since their 1977 divorce had been a civil one, Jewish law did not formally recognize it. In her father's eyes, Shirley and Julius were still married, because Julius had never given Shirley a "get," a bill of divorce.

In response to a dying father's request, the two had agreed to try, and had moved back in together, attempting to return to their lives as husband and wife. They were sincere and made a true effort to grant her father his wish. Shirley really wanted to keep the family together; it was the closest thing to security she'd ever known.

Yet her father died soon thereafter and Shirley found herself slowly slipping back into depression. With her father gone, and a marital relationship in name only, her wide mood swings intensified.

Shirley couldn't cope with even the smallest details of day-to-day existence. Hopelessness overcame her so much that she woke up one day and found herself in a mental hospital, drugged to the hilt. Floating in and out of consciousness, she had no idea how or when she'd gotten to the hospital. One week later Shirley was declared fit for release, yet no answers had been found and there were no indications as to what exactly was at the root of her problem. Clinical depression, chemical imbalance, they called it. Medication was the way to regulate it, advised the doctors.

Shirley needed answers and was determined to find them. Locating a secluded place, she went away for a few days, time needed to desperately try and sort out all that had recently happened to her. What had been the catalyst that caused her to land in a psychiatric hospital?

Sadly, the retreat offered few conclusions and no solutions. With no other options available on her horizon, Shirley admitted she had responsibilities that must be addressed. She couldn't hide away any longer and would have to go on.

Returning to the home she was still sharing with Julius, again relying heavily upon prescription drugs to regulate her emotional existence, Shirley tried to get back into a familiar routine. It did not take long to realize that she and Julius could not live as husband and wife.

He was an honest, good man; he loved her and their children and sincerely wanted to do what was best for his family. Yet, he didn't possess the understanding or patience needed to cope with Shirley's ongoing, deepening depression. It had driven a wedge between them during their earlier years; now it forced them completely apart. Julius, in spite of his efforts, was still unable to reach his troubled wife.

While Shirley desperately tried to salvage her marriage, her sister was suddenly shot. Working to get out of an ugly romantic relationship—with another woman—Shirley's sister was shot by her lover during a domestic argument. It hadn't caused any permanent physical damage, yet it did create overwhelming emotional upheaval, both for her and for the family as a whole.

So Shirley was forced to deal all at once with a barrage of ugly experiences. The prolonged illness and death of her father. Her sister's tumultuous romantic involvement and subsequent shooting. Her own escalating depression and prescription drug dependency. Concern over how her deteriorating health affected her children. And the final, irrevocable breakup of her marriage. Everything came together to push her down even farther into that deep, dark hole she was coming to know all too well.

Shirley left the house and the marriage and moved in with her sister who now had the extra space. Having been in and out of so many institutions—both academic and psychiatric—Shirley had no real home. Still, she had to live somewhere.

Moving in with her sister was a less-than-ideal arrangement. It was, however, better than being homeless, and life did seem to stabilize for a short while. At least for as long as her sister's girlfriend stayed away.

But that situation didn't last very long. In a move that would bode well for no one, the girlfriend made a surprise phone call to Shirley's sister. She cajoled and convinced her that they should meet to discuss their problems. The next thing Shirley knew, the girlfriend had moved back in and she was being unceremoniously booted out.

"Where should I go?" she cried, not believing that her own sister would be so callous.

"I don't care," came the cold response, delivered with not even a hint of sympathy. "I've got a life to lead, too."

Shirley began her own share of unhealthy relationships after her divorce was eventually finalized. These further upset the children. The five of them had dealt, each in his or her own way, with Shirley's emotional illness. Lewis, the oldest, had moved with his father into his new two-bedroom apartment. The house had sold barely a year after the divorce. Marlene joined them shortly thereafter.

The three remaining children, all boys, couldn't live with their father. He no longer had room for all of them. They couldn't live with their mother, either. She had no real home, moved from place to place, and was currently living with a boyfriend whom they didn't like.

Brian was an alcoholic. The children recognized this, even if Shirley chose to ignore it. She went to live with him on a farm sixty-five miles outside of Johannesburg. The three boys ran away.

The children were eventually found and brought back. Soon it was decided that it would be best for them to go to an orphanage, Arcadia Children's Home. Still so young and confused, the boys didn't understand what was happening with their mother. They loved her deeply, yet they knew they couldn't be with her—not right now, anyway.

With the boys settled at the children's home, Shirley and Brian moved to Scottsborough, three hundred seventy-five miles from Johannesburg.

After almost one year, Shirley became aware that Brian was drinking himself into a state of perpetual incoherence. Yet with her own daily intake of tranquilizing drugs, she could only focus on the desperation of her life. She and Brian were cohabiting in a soulless bid to hold onto someone and something. Leaning on each other's illnesses, they both attempted to ignore the reasons for them.

It was all becoming too much. Shirley found herself at a point where she just couldn't take any more. Somewhere in her dulled mind she understood that she was using Brian as yet another excuse, another way to sidestep the real issues in her life. But she couldn't figure out how to make things change. Her marriage had failed, her children were no longer with her, and she was living with an alcoholic who was in as much psychological danger as was she.

Everything Shirley embraced, even Brian, offered her no relief, only creating a stronger yearning somewhere deep inside her heart for something that would permanently alleviate her suffering. The pain kept gnawing away at her, bit by bit, tenuous emotion by tenuous emotion. She was not the woman she was meant to be. Her life had always been a constant search to get beyond the agony. Yet it was always there.

□□□

After the bumpy road with Brian had run its course, Shirley moved in with Peter. Over a short period of time, he showed himself to be in no better condition than his predecessor. More and more, he became a burden as well as an imminent danger to her, physically, mentally, emotionally. Peter was yet another man who had his own deep hurts to resolve. The two of them together were a potentially dangerous combination, but, despite the volatility, they continued to live together.

Shirley had no idea of where to turn to counteract her mounting heartache. Nothing had been right, not since that first day in the convent. No one had ever been able to help her deal with the overwhelming disappointment which was her life.

One day Shirley found herself on the floor, face down, wailing out loud, "God help me, help me!" So much had happened to her. Tragedy and trauma were on the verge of culminating into an overwhelming burden. She was not able to handle life on her own. And she could find no one who could.

There seemed to be no answer. No thunderbolt, no voice from above to respond to her cry.

Once again Shirley found herself in the emergency room of yet another psychiatric hospital. The doctor in charge of her case was alarmed at her hollow stare and the depth of her hopelessness. He was so concerned for her immediate well-being that he admitted her on the spot, stating firmly that she needed some time for complete quiet and rest.

That quiet and rest wasn't to be. Even the slightest things upset Shirley and coping with larger issues was completely beyond her strength. When her daughter, Marlene, was allowed to visit one night, the news she unassumingly brought with her took Shirley to the edge. "Mom," she tried to choose her words carefully, "Peter is gone."

Shirley looked at her daughter as if she didn't comprehend.

"He is gone," Marlene repeated slowly, hoping that the impact of her words would shake her mother out of her apathy. "He's taken all his clothes and left you."

It was hopeless.

Shirley felt unloved. Uncared for. Ignored. Sick. Hurting. She was certain no one understood her; for that matter, no one seemed to want to try.

She knew that she was on a precipice, about to give up—for good. Somehow that realization gave her a small slice of relief. She felt that she would never find the peace she craved. It had always been out of her reach. Truthfully, she was tired of even looking for it.

The search had been futile, fruitless, a waste of precious time. Too much work, and nothing but heartache. There seemed to be only one workable solution.

Suicide.

Chapter Three
GARY

The year was 1951. In Springs, South Africa, thirty miles outside of Johannesburg, Gary Beresford was born. His parents, Ernie and Irene, were English Jews who had married in 1944 during the Second World War. Their immigration to South Africa came in 1948.

During that same year, Israel declared its independence as a self-governing state. Its birth was simultaneously innocent and defiant. The people of this new country were quite certain of what they wanted to achieve, but were just as uncertain as to how to go about accomplishing those goals.

Israel would eventually be the catalyst behind virtually everything Gary Beresford did, said, and worked towards. As an adult, accomplishing the goal of his own immigration to Israel was to become his mission on this earth.

But in 1951, the young country of Israel was of little consequence to Gary or to his parents. They lived with Irene's mother and father in Johannesburg, in a three-bedroom ranch-style home. Willie, Irene's father, was Gary's hero; he was the quintessential English gentleman. Willie always wore a suit, with a collar and tie, and regularly reminded his rapt young grandson, "Gary, when you're rich you can dress any way you want, but when you are poor, dress like you're a millionaire."

The child delighted in the intimate times he spent with his grandfather, who was forever telling him stories of his early life. A soldier in World War I, he regaled young Gary with vivid descriptions of what it had been like to be in the trenches in France during active combat.

Gary fiercely believed every word of what his grandfather told him, for the old man had many physical battle scars to prove his stories. A mustard gas burn on his leg had never healed; Gary learned to watch as his grandfather had it re-dressed daily. An eye had been shot out and, in its place, each day Gary looked adoringly into the glass one.

His grandfather's bravery and good humor, despite the sorrows he had experienced, left an impression on Gary which he never forgot. He recognized in his grandfather a sense of joy that transcended life's trials, a positive outlook that became a bright spot in the young boy's every day. He wanted to learn how to always feel that kind of joy.

In 1956, the extended family moved from Springs to Port Elizabeth, approximately five hundred miles east of Cape Town. Ernie and Irene worked full-time, Ernie as an upholstery manufacturer and Irene as an exceptionally well-known local beautician with a flourishing clientele. Gary was looked after by his grandparents.

This arrangement was ample and comfortable, a lifestyle where physical needs were not a problem. Gary learned to understand the value of money while never having to grapple with the hardships of going without it. His grandfather's admonition to "dress like a millionaire" when he was poor just did not apply to Gary's life. They weren't overly wealthy, yet he never lacked in any material needs.

His spiritual well-being, however, wasn't as closely addressed. His grandparents were loving and attentive, and his attachment to them was strong; yet he did not have a well-defined connection to his parents. This lack created a mixed sense of identity in young Gary. Jewishness, while never denied by his parents nor his grandparents, took a backseat to the day-to-day realities of growing up. Merely a fact of life, it was not really directly addressed.

Gary then grew up receiving mixed emotional signals, ones which didn't leave any real hurts but which caused him to wonder about the role his Jewish heritage should have upon his daily life. Gary took part in the normal teenage happenings around him, attending a public high school as one of only four Jewish students in a class of six hundred.

At about this time, his father's active participation in his life increased greatly as soccer became a shared interest, a common ground between them. Through soccer, they could repeatedly come together and solidify their relationship as father and son.

Gary's father refereed local soccer matches and regularly took him along to see the games. Gary intensely enjoyed watching the sport, and his father as he refereed. The interplay caused Gary's delight to deepen as time passed. On Friday evenings, the two of them left early to claim a good parking space at the soccer grounds in Port Elizabeth and settle in for the upcoming game. It became their ritual. Father-and-son time. It was almost sacred between them.

Yet, despite this growing attachment to his dad, Gary still received no defined religious instruction from him, nor from any of his other family members. When he was twelve his parents declared, "When you get older you can decide what *you* want to be. As of right now, we're Jewish, therefore, you're Jewish." That was that. Yet, despite their admission that they were Jews, Gary's family didn't celebrate any of the traditional Biblical holidays. They rarely went to synagogue. As Gary got older, this lack of involvement didn't change.

Without solid spiritual guidance from any direction, Gary decided he would just have to draw his own conclusions. But he was in no great hurry to do so. Surely there was plenty of time to come face-to-face with that part of life, later on, whenever he would absolutely need to face it.

He knew about God, or at least about the impersonal, general God of whom his mother spoke, and he was content with his Jewish identity in a detached, unconcerned way. It wasn't a driving, all-consuming matter for him. Becoming a teenager, getting involved in and learning about all that was around him, was what mattered the most. Life needed to be lived.

Then Gary's beloved grandfather died of a heart attack, the direct result of a heart weakened years past by rheumatic fever, from which he had never fully recovered. Gary was only thirteen and felt bereft and uncertain of how to continue an existence that had suddenly lost one of its most integral people.

The teenager was suddenly forced to consider life, death, and every accompanying implication.

Was this all there was...a set number of years upon this earth and then...nothing? Nothing at all beyond the grave? Did the depth and breadth of a human life end on a sterile, impersonal bed when the heart stopped functioning? What did it mean?

His grandfather's demise began for Gary an escalating search for reasons behind his own existence. In the years immediately following, he felt a searing need within to look closer at life.

□□□

At sixteen, in December, 1967, his father took him on a trip to Europe and Israel. Just the two of them. Business was partly the reason, but Gary knew that his father was also seeking quality, personal time alone with his son. Their relationship had become close, and his father enjoyed each opportunity for it to grow even closer.

The trip also propelled Gary headlong into the discovery of his Jewish roots. Jerusalem had only recently been liberated from Jordanian rule. Up to this point, few people had seen the sights that Gary and his father were treated to so soon after this liberation.

The Western Wall. The retaining wall of the ancient Temple, the focus of Jewish worship for so many generations. This was not merely a sight, but an experience. Gary learned of the nickname by which this ancient wall had come to be known—"the Wailing Wall." He stood before the huge stones and listened to the "wails"—the strenuous, emotional prayers that could be heard as Jews from all over Israel and the world came to personally reclaim this part of Jewish history for themselves. Gary could sense the breathtaking power and awe which the Wall inspired. The Jordanians, he knew from keeping up with current events, had done everything they could to make the area surrounding the Wall a complete trash dump; since the liberation, the site had been hastily reorganized for the sake of the visitors expected to come. In spite of the attempt to desecrate this spot, the history and intensity of the Wall took one's breath away.

Gary soaked up everything, filing away in his brain facts and bits of history for future rumination. Inspired by each new thing he saw, he somehow knew these sights would eventually mean more to him, putting together the pieces of life's puzzle. He didn't know *how* he knew this, but he was certain of it nevertheless. This was unquestionably his history, too.

In front of the solid, ancient, structure of the Western Wall, Gary's senses were overwhelmed by the magnitude of where he stood and the prayers and presence of the people around him. He closed his eyes and breathed deeply at the thought of the countless others who had been here before him.

There was something beyond this, though, something else he couldn't quite understand. As if a gentle water washed over him,

Gary experienced a comforting and profound sense of spirituality. He couldn't explain in words how or what he felt, yet the experience as a whole imprinted itself into his memory. He determined that, when he returned home to South Africa, he would sincerely attempt to cultivate his spiritual awareness.

The effort to do so was two full years in actualization. When he turned eighteen, beginning to live on his own for the first time in his life, Gary slowly became involved with the Jewish community by joining a local synagogue.

In Port Elizabeth there were three synagogues. One Reform and two Orthodox. He realized that besides choosing between specific synagogues, he also had to select between these two perspectives. Not having a strong knowledge of Judaism as a whole, and unable to read Hebrew, he joined the Reform temple, deciding it would be easier to accustom himself to this atmosphere. As he understood it, being Orthodox meant that he would have to give up more, and be strict in his living arrangements. He wasn't sure he was ready for that.

Through the ensuing years of Gary's association with the Reform Temple in Port Elizabeth, he received an ongoing elementary education in what it meant to be a Jew. He learned about the traditions, the history, the culture. He began to feel a connection with other Jewish people as a whole, and intentionally cultivated Jewish friends.

It was during this time that he joined an all-male organization called the Hebrew Order of David. Founded in the early twentieth century as a "fraternal helping hand" for Jewish immigrants from Eastern Europe resettling in South Africa, its sole purpose had been to make life easier for people coming in from another country. They assisted refugees as they began to learn the language, adjust to a new culture and surroundings, and acquire skills for employment.

By the time Gary joined, the organization had evolved into one whose main aim was that of fundraising for the Jewish community and promoting the Jewish cultural experience in South Africa.

It was the Hebrew Order which helped Gary move within Jewish circles of influence, and offer his professional services to people within these circles. Eventually he became a member of the Management committee and an office-bearer of the local chapter in his home town. The Hebrew Order helped advance Gary's absorption into the life of the Jewish community.

It was also through the Hebrew Order that Gary met his first wife, Melanie.

□□□

He was twenty-one years old, held a decent job, and was active in the local Jewish scene in Port Elizabeth. It was one week before the annual celebration of Purim, the festival initiated in the biblical book of Esther, commemorating the Jews' escape from massacre in the fifth century B.C.E. Gary didn't have a date for the party which was sponsored by the Hebrew Order. To make matters worse, he didn't know of any Jewish girl he could invite. He even considered inviting a gentile.

When he mentioned this to a friend, a sudden, all-out effort was made to find Gary a *Jewish* date. David, a fellow member, had a cousin who wanted to go but had no one to take her. Melanie was introduced to Gary over coffee; they chatted, and he asked if he could take her to the Purim party.

The first date led to dinner, and that dinner led to others. Gary felt an attraction to her. If he read her correctly, she was also interested in him. Despite the fact Melanie was preparing to return to the out-of-town university she attended, they continued to meet. There was a definite sense that this was becoming something more than casual dating.

Both Gary and Melanie were relatively inexperienced in the complexities of romantic involvements. Their relationship was propelled forward mainly by their attraction to each other. They didn't delve into or examine the reasons behind that attraction, or what it was specifically that continued to draw them together.

Eventually, Melanie had to return to the University at Grahamstown, some seventy-five miles northeast of Port Elizabeth. Two weeks after their last date, Gary felt heavy hearted. He missed her being around, and made a spontaneous decision to surprise her with a visit at her dormitory.

She was caught off guard but delighted to see him. They went for a long drive, talking of all that had happened since they'd last seen each other. Chitchat turned into what it had meant to each of them to be apart. They realized that there was, indeed, something happening between them. Even though they still didn't understand it, they didn't want it to end. They began dating each other exclusively, despite the distance between them and despite the undeniable doubts on Gary's part about their relationship.

Six months later, Gary still struggled with that small voice inside his head which told him to wait, to be more careful. Something was nagging at him, warning him that this relationship was not right for Melanie or for him. There was a feeling that there was something—what *was* it?!—*uncomfortable* between them as a couple. They disagreed a lot, had contrasting opinions on almost everything. They came from divergent family backgrounds. Gary and Melanie were both Jewish, but that's where the similarities ended.

Yet Gary reminded himself that they had been going out together for quite some time. Marriage seemed to be the next logical step. Shoving his concerns far back in his mind, he went ahead and asked her to marry him; she agreed. On December 8, 1974, Melanie became Mrs. Gary Beresford.

The newlywed couple moved to Johannesburg. Gary worked as a production manager in a furniture factory. Both he and Melanie were quite active in the development of the Jewish Youth Movement of the Reform synagogues in South Africa. They spent many, many weekends traveling to other towns to chaperone their youth group.

During the week, Melanie stayed at home, concerned and anxious over the economy and growing costs of raising a family. In 1977, Joel, their first child, was born. Preparations had to be made for him to have the ceremonial *Brit Milah*—circumcision—performed.

After asking various Reform rabbis to officiate, Gary and Melanie were unable to find one still interested enough in this Jewish ritual to perform it for them. They were bitter and disappointed. As a last resort, they went to an Orthodox *mohel*, a man trained in the circumcision ceremony.

Gary had since left the Hebrew Order of David, finding that it no longer filled his growing social and spiritual needs. Together with this new slight against his family from the Reform rabbis in the area, he rejected the Reform Movement, concluding that it was no longer able to satisfy his newfound determination to observe the ancient laws of Judaism. He and Melanie discussed their disappointments and concerns. She agreed with Gary that it was time to dig their Jewish roots even deeper.

They energetically embraced Orthodox Judaism. Gary's personal and professional life see-sawed between periods of contentment and uncertainty. He struggled in his work situation to find a position that satisfied him both intellectually and financially. Switching jobs a number of times, he was finally offered an opportunity to set up a small wholesale furniture operation with a partner. An extensive amount of travel would be required to get the business up and running, but it would be a sacrifice he would have to make.

Gary knew that he was neglecting his wife and young son, but he didn't know any other way to fulfill the growing demands of his position without committing time and energy to it. Tension tightened around his personal life. More and more fighting resulted at home as his travel increased and his business responsibilities grew. Remembering the material comforts that characterized his early life, Gary had a deep-seated desire to provide his family a well-to-do lifestyle. It was important that he create a home for them that was financially stable. But he was just as aware that he needed to spend a greater amount of quality time with them to allow for an open line of communication. Pulled in opposite directions, Gary was torn as to how to deal with the escalating pressures that were closing in on him.

He continued to delay dealing with this conflict although he was aware that he should be addressing it. Gary carried on, ignoring Melanie's needs and concerns, and keeping his own frustrations carefully locked away. In response, Melanie became more and more combative.

She found herself a job to nurture some of her own outside interests. Shortly thereafter, Gary dissolved his business partnership and began working for a local, established retail outlet. Things began to look up—perhaps the difficulties Gary had put off dealing with for so long had eventually righted themselves. He was able to be at home more. Their financial security had not been threatened by his change, and his professional move seemed to him to be a way to compromise.

But Gary and Melanie had never really discussed what they needed to make their life together work. There had never been much communication between them. Their relationship had never had depth. For the next few years Gary thought he sensed an improvement in their marriage; but this was an assessment made on his own, not in communion with his wife. Perhaps another child would give the two of them a reason to grow together. Lauren Samantha was born in 1980. Though still not fully confident, he hoped things would be okay.

Still, Gary continued to feel a coldness inside him, an emotional and spiritual void that he couldn't quite define or understand. He was restless. His marriage was better, but it was nowhere near good. He and Melanie existed in the same house together. They raised their children with some sense of cohesiveness, yet he felt out-of-step with her on all other fronts. They rarely talked of anything important. There was no real joy between them.

He couldn't put a name to his uneasiness, though he was certain it existed.

When Gary received an emergency call from his mother informing him that his father lay comatose in a hospital in Harare, Zimbabwe, where they now lived, he and Melanie were forced to pull together as a couple and make a decision on what to do for Gary's parents. Melanie stood by her husband when he said he was going to withdraw money from the bank. She watched as he grabbed his passport from the dresser. She opened the door for him as he left the house, dutifully staying at home with their two children.

Gary drove fourteen hours to be with his father. It was a close call, a harrowing time of emotional upheaval and uncertainty. Gary's father was discovered to have diabetes. With medication, he was brought out of the coma and eventually was sent home. Gary remained with his parents a few more days after the return, helping them settle back into the routine of homelife. He used this time also to have a look around the city of Harare.

Gary observed the racial unrest in Zimbabwe. A black man had recently been elected to the country's highest office. Political and racial tensions were on the rise, and the cost of living subsequently reached an all-time low. Most of the white people had suddenly vacated the area. Large, beautiful homes in topnotch condition were available for sale way below market value.

He was very impressed with the beauty of the countryside. Politics didn't concern him; he gave the racial problems little thought. Returning home in a renewed and excited state, he asked Melanie if she'd consider moving to Zimbabwe. Her response was immediate and firm. Without any discussion, she declared that she wouldn't even entertain the idea. Never would she leave South Africa. She didn't address his excitement, nor give him room to express his appreciation of Zimbabwe. Her answer was simply, "Not interested."

Gary walked away from the one-sided discussion lower than

he'd ever been. Surely there was no purpose to his life—not in any of the professional efforts he'd attempted, nor in this soulless marriage. He couldn't even find the smallest satisfaction in where he lived.

Gary didn't know where these feelings of discontent came from, exactly what caused them to roil around inside and eat at him, never fully leaving him alone. He would find out, though. No matter the cost, he was determined that he must continue to search until he found peace.

He felt Melanie pushing him farther and farther away. He knew she was aware of his rising discontent, but he felt no empathy coming from her, no help or understanding. Their relationship slipped even farther into the danger zone, precariously close to drowning the mire of resentment Melanie was harboring. Her pent-up anger butted up against his own obvious discontent. Gary didn't know how to get through to her, to tap into the love she once had for him. He couldn't explain his confusion, any of it, even to himself.

Gary knew they had a very serious problem. Melanie knew it, too. Both so caught up in their own misery, neither could see the hurt they were causing each other.

Arguments became fierce and combative. Constantly battling over anything and everything, no matter how big or small, shouting became the only way they addressed one another. Gary proceeded to immerse himself in business, his intense energy fueled by disillusionment. This added to his time away from home. He spent a good majority of his days—and nights—visiting outlying towns for various professional reasons.

□ □ □

In December, 1981, Gary and Melanie made a decision, together, to visit both of their families. Their daughter Lauren had been born in the summer of that year and the grandparents had not yet met their new grandchild. First they would go to Gary's parents' home in Harare, Zimbabwe. It would be a "family" trip. They had finally talked, *really* talked, and agreed that something had to be done to see if they could salvage their marriage. Their situation could not continue as it had. They designed the trip as a time for everyone to relax, to become reacquainted, to enjoy being together. A time, maybe, of marital reunification.

Once again it was a fourteen-hour drive before they reached Harare. Gary's parents were thrilled to see them, though they sensed the strain between their son and his wife. Nonetheless, the visit with his parents was therapeutic for Gary. He and Melanie had gotten that far without reverting to the intensity of their previous discord. At least they were able to maintain an uneasy truce.

They piled back in the car for another fourteen hours, stopping in Johannesburg before going on to see Melanie's parents in Port Elizabeth. With the stop, this leg of the trip added over ten more hours to their time on the road.

By the time they reached Melanie's parents home, they were exhausted and low-spirited; finally their tempers snapped. Though this trip had been the very tool with which they had hoped to mend their relationship, the pressure of the long journey had, instead, reignited their hostilities toward one another. With hope of reconciliation now blown away, Gary and Melanie felt as if they had failed themselves, and each other.

To add to this, money was growing tight. Their finances had dwindled to near nothing. Gary needed a job where he would finally attain financial security. This increased the friction between him and Melanie. They just couldn't seem to find the right combination of financial security and emotional stability between them to make their marriage click.

This was yet another pressure on top of all the others. It weighed on Gary's mind night and day. He felt as if his whole life were closing in on him. He was trying, in his own, faulty human way, to make things work. But he couldn't find the right mix.

The responsibility of making his family a success burdened him down.

Returning from their road trip, homelife reverted to what it had been before they left. One morning Gary went to Vereeniging on a business trip, about thirty miles south of where he and Melanie lived. It was a day that seemed as if it would never end. He pushed himself to the limit to get his work done, returning home later than usual.

It was ten o'clock at night when Gary drove up in front of the house; odd, he thought, noticing that it was completely dark. It was early for Melanie to be in bed, but Gary gave it little consideration. She must've had a trying day with the children.

His key in the front door lock, Gary pushed open the door and flipped on the hall light. When his eyes adjusted, he was shocked to see that the curtains had been taken down and there was no furniture left in the dining room. His steps were slow and full of dread as he walked into the living room. In horror, he discovered that it, too, was bare. The entire house was empty.

In his bedroom, he found only a pillow and a blanket. A lonely towel hung on the bathroom rack, and his clothes were untouched in his closet.

Everything else was gone. Everything!

Melanie had taken their children, their belongings, the sum total of their entire life together, and walked out on him. Gary knew things had been desperate. He had certainly been painfully aware of the tension. He realized that they had for a long time been on the verge of a separation. But for her to just leave with no notice! No advance explanations? He had *not* expected this. He dropped down to the floor and sat there for a long time. How could he have not seen this coming? How could he have been so blind?

Chapter Four

GARY & SHIRLEY

He was hot. Tired. He'd had about enough. And, to make a bad situation worse, the area looked like the most depressing place on the face of God's earth. That was saying volumes, considering some of the locations he'd already examined, to find a place to live, in the course of this dreary, downcast day.

Gary Beresford was isolated and alone. Melanie and the children were gone. Their house was empty. His marriage was dead.

It had happened only yesterday and it still didn't seem real to him. After he'd literally picked himself up off the floor from the shock, he promised himself that he would never live in that house again. After a series of frantic phone calls to try and find out where Melanie had taken the children, he located them at her sister's house. Not surprisingly, she refused to speak with him, indicating through her sister that it was too late in their relationship to begin talking now. Simply put, it was over.

Gary had spent the night at the house; he'd had nowhere else to go at such a late hour. But now, here he was, having spent the last several hours driving around Berea, a suburb of Johannesburg, staring at tedious-looking high rise buildings, desperate to find somewhere new to call home.

He was fulfilling his promise to himself to stay out of the house he'd shared with Melanie. She let him know that he was welcome to it, but he knew the memories contained within would be far too painful. The once-pleasing sounds of the kids playing would echo through those long halls. The uncontrollable sounds of his voice raised in anger at Melanie would permeate the strangled air as ringing accusations. The ugly sounds of her words in response would bounce back at him off the walls, continuing to wound him. It would be too hard to face, day after day. Those recollections, and many, many more, would be an intolerable reminder of what was no longer, of what he'd lost.

No, he couldn't live there anymore, so he spent this entire day on the task of relocation. Before him now stood a possible candidate for new living quarters, a huge high-rise with the appearance of a concrete tower—foreboding, cold, unyielding— sporting a sign on the front lawn: "residential hotel." If it was not exactly warm and welcoming, at least it appeared respectable enough, and Gary was tired of looking. He hoped there was a place here for him to find a much-needed rest.

Once inside the lobby, he waited as a short lady beyond her middle years, white hair and lively eyes, finally appeared from the back office. He introduced himself and, in a voice filled with barely suppressed hope, requested a room for an indefinite period of time.

"Sorry, sir, I only have something available for one week. The hotel is fully booked right now for long-term rentals."

Gary considered his situation and the mounting pressures that he would certainly face in the coming days. With guarded optimism, he accepted the offered room, whether it be for one night or for many. He needed a place to sleep and he needed it now. He'd worry about everything else later. Carrying with him little more than the clothing on his back, Gary was also running out of money. He was in no position to be picky.

Filling out a registration form, Gary took the key the lady handed him, thanked her, and rode the elevator upstairs to his new "home."

□□□

Time seemed lost to him and before long, Gary's week was up. He had spent that time alternately going to work and, in the latter part of his exhausting days, visiting Melanie who was still staying with her sister. Gary implored her to try and work out their differences. He wanted to keep the marriage together, such as it was, for the sake of their children.

But Melanie was determined to go through with this total separation. The effort to reason with her was futile. Gary just didn't have enough emotional energy left to fight anymore. Admitting that a reconciliation would not happen, he hired an attorney after Melanie had filed for a divorce.

The complications of these legal proceedings were now added to the job of finding a permanent place to live. He dreaded resuming the search and hoped instead that something had opened up at the residential hotel.

On the first day of the new week, Gary approached the front office and the lady whom he now knew as Mrs. Levinson.

"Do you by any chance have another room available, one where I could stay on indefinitely?" He knew he wore his hope on his expectant face.

Mrs. Levinson seemed to be aware that he'd been having a hard time and had even offered a few commiserating remarks designed to make him feel better. Her words of kindness went a long way.

She looked into Gary's expectant face as he awaited the verdict.

Finally, she smiled and winked.

"You know what, Mr. Beresford?" Her grin was mischievous. "I've just been told that someone will be moving out this afternoon. You can have her room. Stay as long as you need."

Gary laughed in relief, nearly collapsing against the counter. Good news for a change. "I'll take it. I'll take it! And, what's more," he felt the life flow back into him as he jokingly added, "you can throw in a blonde!" He was surprised at himself as soon as he made the impulsive comment.

Mrs. Levinson, however, took it in stride and laughed right along with him. "My daughter, Shirley, is moving into the hotel tomorrow." She nodded. "I'll introduce her to you. How's that?"

Gary hadn't figured on such a response. A bit flustered at this turn in their conversation, he smiled nervously, nodded, and thanked Mrs. Levinson; yes, of course he'd be pleased to meet her daughter tomorrow. That sounded like a wonderful idea. Nothing would come of it, he told himself as he walked away, but his manners overrode his thoughts. Mrs. Levinson had been very good to him this past week. Meeting her daughter was the least he could do in return, if indeed, she was serious. Or was she only joking, responding to his giddy remark?

At breakfast the next morning in the hotel dining room, he discovered that Mrs. Levinson hadn't simply been making idle, entertaining conversation the day before.

"Shirley's due at eleven this morning," she told Gary. "Would you be willing to help her move in?"

Shirley. Her daughter. It was Sunday and he really had nothing to do. He could offer his services for a short time. What would it hurt?

"Sure, I'll be glad to help."

When the bellhop informed him a few hours later that Mrs. Levinson's daughter had arrived and was in the hotel parking garage, Gary dutifully went down to introduce himself. As he came closer to her car and saw her for the first time, he hoped his face didn't mirror his surprise. Sure enough, he thought, a blonde. Attractive even.

She watched him approach and, as he came near, he smiled at how her raised eyebrow betrayed her curiosity.

"Hello," he greeted her. "My name is Gary Beresford. I've spoken to your mother and she's asked me to help the bellhop with your belongings."

□□□

As the man came closer, Shirley realized that she was his destination. It hadn't taken him long to introduce himself and, in doing so, he answered her unspoken question.

Ah, my *mother*, Shirley thought. She's sent someone to meet me, trying to run my life for me again. She felt a twinge of resentment, yet somehow she was also releived

"Good," she responded. "My name is Shirley. You can start by removing everything from the back seat of my car and taking it all up to my room."

She noticed Gary's eyes widen at her demand. Perhaps her request had been a bit curt, she realized, but it'd been a long, tiring day and she wasn't in the mood for apologies. After all, he was here because her mother asked him to move her luggage upstairs. Next time, she told herself, she would remember the pleasantries. However, this time, he'd have to do without them.

Gary did as she requested without comment. He was sure, though, that Shirley could read the thoughts moving through his head. She gave him a little shrug, and he took a deep breath in response. They stared at each other for one brief moment, then Gary began collecting her belongings and removing them from the car. He could feel his lips tighten in his attempt to hold back his natural response. Some things are best left unsaid, he told himself. He'd had enough arguing of late.

He could feel her move silently right behind him as she

followed up the stairs. Once everything was deposited in her room, little time was spent on chitchat. Gary was determined to cut short this meeting. Had it happened under less tense circumstances, perhaps their meeting might have been pleasant. As it was, the air here was too chilly for him. He left her alone.

□□□

Shirley sighed deeply, surveying her new surroundings. These last few days, here in the apartment building her mother managed, had been tedious and sad. She moved restlessly about her room, her new "home." Softly fingering the few comforting knick-knacks she had brought with her, her eyes blurred with unexpected tears. Sitting on the edge of her bed, Shirley reflected on the turns her life had recently taken, considering all that had transpired since her father had died. Her marriage had died, too. She wiped away sudden tears as she recalled the disastrous turns her life had taken since then.

She had seriously considered suicide—it had seemed her only alternative. The thought filled her once again with fear. Strange, how Marlene's stark words informing her of Peter's disappearance had somehow shaken her out of her apathy. Those words, "He's left you," had been a turning point.

She had a nebulous idea that there was a God somewhere, and he had intervened, releasing her from each of her destructive relationships. He had taken an otherwise bad situation and worked it into what *could* become a productive one. Here she was now, and it was time to make the best of it.

Shirley shook her head to clear it of the memories, still fresh, painful, raw. She realized that she had been sitting on the bed for some time, simply staring off into space. What was she doing? There were things that needed taking care of and she had spent far too many precious moments dwelling on and mourning the past. It was time to change.

She looked around her room and grimaced as she examined her surroundings. The differences between this and the house where she and Julius had lived were vast. Their home had been extraordinarily beautiful, a ranch-style structure with a swimming pool and a lovely garden. Expensive furnishings. Material comfort at her fingertips.

But, she nodded resolutely, standing up and walking to a window, that was gone and she had to get used to what was here. This was her new reality and there were things she could do to make it more comfortable and homey.

Needlepoint was her favorite pastime, a soothing hobby which had helped her through many rough spots. She'd framed many of her works over the years. Glancing around, she noticed that her tapestries, carelessly hung over various pieces of furniture, had been ignored since the day she had first brought them in. As long as she was to be here for an indefinite period, Shirley decided to make the room as attractive as possible. The tapestries needed to be on the walls. But she needed help to put them there.

Until now Shirley had given little thought to the man who'd helped her move in. Taking hold of the phone receiver, she dialed the front desk. "Hello, this is Mrs. Shirley Weinstein. That man my mother sent to help me when I came here, that Gary? Can you give me his room number?"

Number in hand, she then dialed Gary's room. "Hello," she said, "this is Shirley."

□ □ □

Actually, Gary was quite surprised to hear Shirley's voice when he picked up the phone. He hadn't really expected to hear from her again. Well, he thought, perhaps I made an impression on her majesty after all. His smile broadened as he waited for her to continue speaking.

"Would you like to come upstairs again and help me hang some tapestries?" she asked. "Maintenance will give you a hammer and nails."

Gary was too stunned to respond. Once more, her nerve amazed him. Was he supposed to be available to her every whim? Despite his mixed feelings, he agreed to help her.

Slowly, cautiously, over the course of the next few weeks, he and Shirley became friends. He grew accustomed to how abrupt she could be, and she found his company comfortable enough to enable her to relax and open up. Neither was looking for any kind of romantic involvement; however, each was delighted to find in the other a trusting, caring confidante.

Chapter Five

LOVE & MARRIAGE

In early 1982, Gary's divorce was proceeding, but the process was difficult and excruciatingly painful. The estate he had shared with his estranged wife became the object of a bitter battle. Being separated from his children for long periods of time was almost more than he could stand. Once again, his emotions were pulled in every direction.

Through it all, Shirley was there, right next to him. Gary knew, from their long and intimate talks together, that she, too, was dealing with a list of her own hurts. She herself had been as desperate as a person can become.

Still, Shirley had managed to pull herself up, and was always available to lend a sympathetic ear to his concerns. Willingly, she offered a friendly, comforting shoulder to help bear his burden, one which continually threatened to topple him. Shirley was a confidante who understood, from personal experience, how difficult life could be.

However, the last thing that Gary needed was another serious involvement. He cautiously kept his distance, continuing their alliance through a thinly-veiled curtain he called friendship. He knew she was seeing other men. He felt it was better to keep their relationship from becoming too clearly defined.

Gary was delighted to spend large chunks of time with her, to talk and commiserate, to watch the way her face always lit up when they were together. Still, he drew the line at any specific, in-depth emotional entanglement, for the pain of his marriage was still too fresh. He could not forget the way his ex-wife had abandoned their union without a backward glance. Was he ready to become involved with another woman?

Gary didn't think so.

However, his heart had its own agenda. Time rolled by and his relationship with Shirley had to go somewhere. It refused to sit idly by on the sidelines, even though it as yet had no focus. He felt himself attracted to her as a friend is drawn to a friend, in addition to experiencing the natural affections a man feels toward a woman. When he first began to seriously consider the implications of these complex and warring emotions, when he dared to think of how very appealing he found Shirley, he automatically and forcefully rebelled.

How could he allow for the possibility of an involvement beyond what they now had? How could he take that chance and risk another awful failure? When he was with her at these times, Gary knew that he became obnoxious, difficult, even rudely inconsiderate; he realized he was acting badly. He didn't really want to push her away—in all honesty, he could no longer imagine life without her—but neither could he seem to get a handle on these automatic, negative defense mechanisms. He didn't know how to deal with the push-pull struggle inside of him.

One day his emotions began to boil anew. Reacting as usual,

he lashed out at Shirley in a careless way. Immediately, Gary observed her hurt, wounded expression. The sight of the sadness as it clouded her expressive face, revealed how deeply cutting his words had been. Seeing the look of naked pain in her eyes was too much to watch, and he abruptly turned away. Gary was filled with self-loathing; he couldn't stand to know his words and actions could make her so unhappy.

He was thoroughly ashamed. But his shame helped him see what he would be throwing away if this disastrous attitude was allowed to continue. Everything became excruciatingly clear, but he needed time to think.

Either something must change, he decided, or I'll just have to sever this relationship. Gary realized he couldn't allow his own needs and hurts to cause Shirley further heartache. From all that she had related about her life, it was clear that this woman had already experienced enough disappointment and pain. Gary refused to allow himself to become the source of further anguish.

Shirley, too, recognized the motivation for the change in Gary's behavior. It was clear that he was trying to construct an impenetrable wall to guard against further emotional hurt. Yet she never once let this deter her from continuing to be his friend. She stayed close by, and was always there when he needed a good, loyal companion.

This amazed him. It also petrified him. Obviously she had found something worthwhile in him. Difficult as it was, he had to accept the dawning realization that he needed Shirley Weinstein. Deeply touched by her loving, gentle spirit, Gary did want her to be there for him; he also wanted the chance to offer her the same abiding comfort.

The thought of losing her became even more frightening than the knowledge that keeping her would require new, serious commitments. He'd also have to change some of his old habits. No longer could Gary turn and run from his problems. He would somehow have to learn to communicate more freely.

When they next met, well after Gary had engaged in a considerable amount of personal reflection, he sensed a subtle difference in Shirley. More certain of what he wanted, she, in turn, also appeared calmer, more open. It was as if she realized that things had changed in his mind. Shirley seemed to personally sense his moods and to know what he was thinking.

He dared to give himself permission to express a tiny portion of his growing affection and Shirley wholeheartedly, without reservation, accepted it and reciprocated. Gary watched in amazement as Shirley blossomed under his careful courtship. He was surprised and delighted every day as he felt himself grow more confident and at ease with his life as a result of her gentle concern.

By June, 1982, his divorce was finalized. Yet Gary still felt the turmoil and strain. His bitterness wasn't only reserved for his ex-wife and what they had just been through. His lawyers had proven themselves to be incompetent and self-serving; he could do nothing about it.

The lawyers, in fact, had been the *only* winners in the torturous battle. Gary had gone through two attorneys in his painstaking efforts to reach a satisfactory divorce settlement. To appear in court in South Africa, one needed not only a lawyer but also an advocate briefed by the lawyer. Gary's first attorney and advocate proved absolutely useless, confusing rather than helping the situation.

Shirley offered him the name of a second firm of attorneys. While this group was an improvement over his original counsel, the ultimate outcome was far from satisfactory. Gary found that not only had he been forced to turn over nearly all his financial assets to his ex-wife, but also to the professionals who were supposed to protect him.

Even more excruciating than the financial sacrifice he sustained, was the loss of regular contact with his beloved children. Gary didn't know if he'd ever fully recover from that constant pain. Conscious that he would be forced to forfeit many of the opportunities full-time fathers enjoy as they experience the daily triumphs and sadnesses of their children, Gary grieved.

No longer would he experience their day to-day thrills—a stellar report card, a sports achievement, a party invitation; nor would he always be around on the spur of the moment to help them get over the normal disappointments of growing up—skinned knees, feuds with friends, bad dreams. He would become a visiting father.

Though she could not take the place of his family, Gary was grateful each new day for Shirley. She was there for him, to help fill the void that the time away from his children created.

Yet the growing feelings he felt for her continued to frighten him, even more than the court case. He didn't want to care intimately for Shirley. He didn't want to fall in love again. Not with Shirley, not with anyone.

His previous experience with commitment and marriage had taught him that love brought nothing but pain, anguish, and deceit. He couldn't stand all that again. He wouldn't subject himself to that another time. Neither did he ever again want to contribute to someone else's hurt.

He decided to approach Shirley with his rising concerns. It would be callous and unfair to lead her on and make her think their relationship would ever be more. He wanted to be honest with this woman who had, up to now, proven herself to be worthy of nothing less.

It was a beautiful night. They'd gone to dinner. Driving home, Gary's voice came out of the still quiet, making her turn to him expectantly.

"I'm not sure where we're going with our relationship," he began firmly.

"Neither am I."

"I care for you so much, Shirley. I enjoy our time together. I feel there could be much more but, well, that thought frightens me."

"I know, Gary. I'm scared, too."

Gary's eyebrow raised and he stole a surprised glance her way. It had never occurred to him that what was happening between them could create uneasiness for Shirley, as well as for him. He was new to this kind of easy, giving interplay.

She smiled. "I guess you never thought of it like that, did you?"

Gary returned her grin. "Actually, no. I only saw my concerns. It really never crossed my mind that you might be thinking along the same lines. I didn't dare to hope."

"Are we talking about similar feelings here, Gary? Are we both considering the same intensity of involvement?"

The conversation proceeded. They spoke their thoughts, they revealed their fears. Finally, issue by issue, they considered together what had for months dominated their individual thoughts separately.

They discussed at length Gary's concerns and Shirley's responses to those concerns. They examined Shirley's personal hesitance about entering into another relationship. They discussed what to do to try and overcome the fears that events in their individual lives had caused.

Gradually, Gary began to feel that it might work. He was now more aware of Shirley's past despair and how those years of confusion had caused her intense, ongoing emotional and physical difficulties. He learned of her medications and hospitalizations.

None of that changed his mind or made any difference to him. He, in turn, revealed his own blemishes, and marveled as Shirley graciously accepted them. They were good for each other. The possibilities of a life together grew wonderful to consider. He and Shirley delighted in a newfound excitement over what the future might hold for them.

Allowing only a small bubbling spring of hope at first, just a trickle of happiness, they soon permitted a steady flow of joy to wash over them.

Gary was surprised to realize that one of the strengths of their relationship was their easy communication. The crucial element that had been missing from his relationship with Melanie was present between him and Shirley. He treasured and anticipated the times they spent simply talking to each other.

He cautiously stepped out beyond his hurt. It could work. It really *could.* He knew now that he wanted to spend the rest of his life with Shirley.

In July of 1982, Gary and Shirley moved out of the residential apartment building, renting a cottage on a farm outside of Johannesburg. On September 12th they were married in an Orthodox synagogue in Johannesburg. Eyes open, they went into their union, dedicating themselves to new lives. Together.

□□□

It was the start of the first real brightness both Gary and Shirley had ever known, even despite the lingering, stubborn shadows that followed behind them. Melanie had begun to pressure Gary both financially and emotionally. Shirley was continually plagued by uncertainties and lingering resentments towards her mother. Try as she might, she couldn't rid herself of these ancient grudges. Her time in the convent, and the following years of frantic hopelessness, were hard memories to shake.

It was with all this in mind that they considered a move, a fresh start in a different place. As they had each done separately in the past when coming to a life passage, as a couple they wanted to begin again in a brand new location. They felt they owed it to each other to create every available opportunity for their marriage not only to last, but to prosper.

Gary's parents still lived in Zimbabwe and he had never forgotten how much he had liked the country. There were benefits there for each of them, both geographically and professionally. At the end of each day, he and Shirley would talk late into the night about moving to Zimbabwe. It was agreed that they would first arrange to visit Gary's parents. His parents hadn't yet met Shirley and it seemed a good time to deal with both concerns.

As a sideline business, Gary had for a few years employed freelance salespeople to sell various Christmas trinkets. Perfume, musical boxes, scarves, and miscellaneous items were annually marketed in many different locations. This offered Gary added regular income.

When he and Shirley agreed definitely to make the trip to Zimbabwe, Gary brought along a trunk full of trinkets available for sale. His market research had determined that these goodies would likely sell there because the country presently had a shortage of gift items and other such products.

That deficiency in the Zimbabwean economy turned out to be a professional and financial windfall for Gary and Shirley. People had money to buy with but the government was not allowing the goods to flow freely to the people.

Thus, when Gary and Shirley showed up, offering an array of hard-to-get Christmas presents out of the trunk of their car, they sold the entire stock within four days, netting a significant amount of money. This profit, it was determined, would provide the down payment on the purchase of a home there in Zimbabwe. Shirley also loved it there and they both knew it was the perfect place for them to relocate.

They were aware that, to many people, it might seem foolish to move so abruptly, without first making certain that they could sustain themselves in the new country. They weren't Zimbabwean citizens, nor did they possess resident status or work permits. Yet Gary's skills in marketing had already showed he could be successful. And they felt some guiding force leading them into this decision. They were certain that it was the right move for them to make.

They went ahead and proceeded to shop for a house. It wasn't long before they found their dream home—a spacious place on two acres of land in the bustling, exciting cosmopolitan city of

Harare. They put down a deposit and, in only two weeks, their mortgage application was approved.

Mortgage available, house awaiting them, and money in the bank, still neither Gary nor Shirley had yet received a work permit. The appropriate paperwork had been filed. They needed to act quickly. The rental lease was up on their cottage outside of Johannesburg, and the house in Harare was now theirs, ready for occupancy. This seemed the perfect time to make the transition.

Since they had moved so decisively to leave South Africa, it was truly too late to change their minds. Nor did they want to. They went ahead with plans as scheduled, returning briefly to South Africa to pack their belongings. They were bound for their new home in Harare, with or without work permits. It would all work out. They had faith that it would.

□□□

The permits came through without any problems, soon after they settled into their new house. Gary was able to secure a position as Group Marketing Manager for a company involved in manufacturing office furniture and alternative energy equipment. Shirley obtained a job as a manager of a local gallery specializing in Zimbabwean-produced art. Married life suited them perfectly.

They fulfilled each other emotionally and, financially, they began to amass wealth by trading in porcelain and fine art. Gary had a three-year contract with his company with an option to renew. They anticipated settling in Zimbabwe for an indefinite period of time. As persons of British nationality, they had the right to live as citizens in England or any European Economic Community country. Feeling that they would eventually move, for now they were happy where they were.

Zimbabwe was a country steeped in old colonial tradition. Gary and Shirley were comfortable with the societal structure of Harare and became part of the Jewish "in-crowd." They joined the local

Jewish country club, regularly playing tennis and getting involved in various community functions.

In the evenings, from the veranda of the house they had come to love and enjoy, they watched the sun set, wrapping themselves comfortably in the peace and colorful natural beauty of their surroundings amidst the African bush country.

Although Gary had reinstated his membership in the Hebrew Order of David in Harare, his mind was more preoccupied with the sweet, well-padded life he now knew. Most of the members at the country club also belonged to the Hebrew Order. It was an accepted, even expected, part of the Jewish community fabric.

He wasn't paying much more than lip service to his actual Jewishness, with little conscious consideration for his spirituality. The Hebrew Order helped to fill his social and professional needs, but didn't mean much else.

He was a Jew. Shirley was a Jew. That's what they were. Period. It was a nice existence these days. Being Jewish didn't give them much pause for thought. Beyond the occasional visit to synagogue, being Jewish offered them an established, solid identity, and a well-placed position in their local community.

Their world had, for the most part, righted itself better than either of them had ever expected for themselves. Gary and Shirley Beresford thought they had finally found what they'd always been looking for.

They were secure.

□□□

It was 1984. Shirley longed to visit her family in Israel whom she had not seen in many years, so she and Gary agreed to take a holiday. Gary had been there several times before. Shirley had not.

Her aunt, Hannah, lived in Afula, a small town situated in the central part of the country. Excruciatingly hot and humid, Afula seemed a primitive location to the Beresfords. Used to civilization and the daily extras of a materially-privileged life, Shirley found what she saw in that tiny village, stark and unappealing.

Aunt Hannah lived in a minuscule, one-bedroom structure of unknown vintage. Shirley was certain, from her first look at the house, that it had never been anything but a box in which people lived. The floor was shrouded in a linoleum pattern, at least thirty years old; the walls exhibited a faded, depressing wallpaper. Furniture, undoubtedly of the same era as the linoleum, seemed to be discarded odds and ends placed haphazardly wherever they fit. At least it was clean and respectable.

Modern conveniences, such as a roomy, well-equipped bathroom, were nothing less than a deserved necessity in Shirley and Gary's world back in Zimbabwe. Here, the bathroom made one feel claustrophobic. In it was a washing machine that restricted the use of the rest of the room space. The toilet, when it could be reached beyond the washing machine, worked only if a specific, complicated set of steps were taken to flush it. A shower? Only a hose-like hand-held sprayer. Bathtub? None.

The entire experience tried their patience to its limits. Gary felt quietly uncomfortable; Shirley, however, was overwhelmingly vocal about her disgust with everything Israel represented. By the time their visit had ended and she was comfortably seated aboard the airplane which would take them back to Zimbabwe, she had seen more than enough.

Turning to her husband, she announced adamantly, "Gary, that was worse than a third-world country!" Their plane was off the runway and the Israeli landscape fell behind them. "If that place," she disgustedly waved her hand toward the window and land below, "is Israel, get me away! I can't stand it, and I'd *never* live there!"

Chapter Six

THE CALLINGS

One evening, after returning to Zimbabwe, Gary and Shirley sat at home watching television when the phone rang. Upon completing a brief conversation, Shirley returned to the living room, smiling broadly.

"Who was that, love?"

"Rose Leon," Shirley responded, cozily sitting down next to her husband.

Rose was the wife of one of their tennis friends from the country club. She had called to ask Gary and Shirley over for a Friday night "*kabbalat Shabbat*" meal, the meal traditionally eaten by Jews at the beginning of the Sabbath. Another couple, the Mellers, were also invited.

Shirley accepted the invitation and set about the task of finding out more about Don and Freda Mellers, people whom neither she nor Gary knew very well. After talking to a Jewish friend, Shirley reported to Gary that the Mellers were considered to be "Jesus freaks." The Beresfords thought little of that, believing in "live and let live." It didn't matter to them what others believed.

Friday evening arrived and the Beresfords went to the Leons' house for dinner. Along with the Mellers, another couple was in attendance. The eight of them had a lovely, pleasant evening. Conversation was general, but Gary did notice his wife spending a good deal of time in close conversation with Freda Meller.

On the drive home, after a period of comfortable silence, Shirley stated, "Freda needs my help."

"Oh?" Gary kept his eyes on the road, but his voice indicated his interest.

"I think she should develop a more positive outlook on life. She seems very happy but, well, things can always get better."

It was obvious to Gary that Shirley and Freda had gotten on well. Shirley had joined the ever-growing "positive thinking" movement awhile back, when she'd been at the lowest point in her depression. Though it had never fully satisfied her needs, her outlook on life had evened out, especially since their marriage. She recognized that this movement wasn't a cure-all but, she still enjoyed sharing her thoughts on it with others, especially those with whom she felt a special rapport.

Gary knew that his wife identified strongly with anyone whom she thought harbored feelings of unfulfillment. Shirley might have sensed this during her time spent with Freda. Life in the convent and the discouraging , disappointing years that followed had created in Shirley a deep longing for something to ground her, to offer her permanent meaning. She was forever looking.

Even though Shirley had successfully emerged from the deepest pits of despair, emotionally she was still somewhat delicate. Knowing the horrors of depression, she was committed to helping others overcome similar problems. She thought she found in Freda a kindred spirit.

A few days later, Freda called and invited them to their house for the evening. Upon arriving, Gary and Shirley were greeted warmly and, over coffee and cookies, the couples chatted about general topics, slowly learning more about one another.

Freda leaned in towards Shirley. With her eyes on both Shirley and Gary, she asked quietly, "Have you two ever heard about 'the Jewish Messiah'?"

"You mean Jesus Christ?" Gary responded, not sure of where this was going. Without awaiting verification, he continued, "Of course we've heard of the man. Who hasn't?"

"Yes," Don interjected, "but do you know why, after all these years, he still means so much to so many people, and how he is especially important to the Jews?"

The *Jewish* Messiah? The Beresfords looked at each other with amused curiosity. The conversation had taken on unexpected dimensions. Not that they necessarily resented the direction, but they both felt as if it would be a waste of a good visit.

Don and Freda, despite the Beresfords' expressions of exaggerated patience, eagerly related their own personal stories of how they had come to know this Jesus. They talked of him as if he were their best friend. Their eyes lit up and their voices filled with a barely-contained emotion when they told of how Jesus, the Messiah, had brought them out of a hopeless existence to give them purpose and direction. Still amazed, the Mellers were genuinely in awe of what this person—who, they claimed, was also the son of God—had done for them.

The Mellers were a caring, pleasant couple who obviously believed what they had shared without reservation. Their hearts were in their every syllable. Gary and Shirley appreciated the comforting words and the obvious feeling behind their deep-rooted faith and strong convictions. Giving their new friends credit for holding such an unshakable belief in something—or someone—so intangible, still, the Beresfords had to gently tell Freda and Don that they didn't identify with this ideology. Their lives, after all, were very good now. They had already come out of their own hopeless existence, separately and together, and had done so without any outside help. They had no need for a messiah, Jewish or otherwise.

Despite her lack of interest in the Meller's messiah, some of Shirley's early memories were revived by Freda's words. Recalling the loneliness and isolation of her childhood and the turmoil of her first marriage, Shirley thought of the crucifix at the convent, and her childish curiosity about the man that hung on it. She could certainly identify with Freda's need to search for a deeper meaning to life.

Shirley suddenly sensed that she herself would always be searching, no matter how comfortable her life became. Life, she decided, would always be a struggle to fill the needs of her heart. She recalled another time, when another friend, a gentile minister, had suggested to her that this same Jesus could heal her wounds and help her find permanent, everlasting peace. What Freda and Don had shared with them was, for her, a ringing reminder.

Yet this was the first time either Gary or Shirley had heard *Jews* speak of a belief in or acceptance of Yeshua, Jesus, as Messiah. Gary's intellect was fascinated by this unusual concept; Shirley's emotions were strangely drawn. With an interest they refused to acknowledge, they absorbed what the Meller's tried to explain to them, asking questions in the process. Gary and Shirley both admitted that they enjoyed the exchange of ideas.

The Beresfords did not feel threatened by what they heard, nor was there any coercion from the Mellers to alter their present belief system. It became, instead, an ongoing, thought-provoking, and stimulating topic of conversation between the two couples. It added an intriguing dimension to their developing relationship.

Over the course of the next few weeks, the four talked more, even reviewing Scripture together. Gary was impressed by a passage in the *Tenach*, the "Jewish Bible" or "Old Testament," which spoke of an "anointed one," a Messiah. His thoughts kept returning to a specific passage in the book of Daniel. Deeply moved, Gary repeatedly asked, "Who *is* this Messiah about whom Daniel wrote?" He was most affected by Daniel's prediction, found in chapter 9, at verse 26, that the Messiah would be "cut off," or killed before Jerusalem was laid waste, and the Temple destroyed. This took place in the year 70. Time-wise, Jesus fit that description. But did that really prove anything?

In the interim, Shirley was spending more and more time with Freda. One afternoon after returning from an outing, she cautiously approached her husband.

"I have to tell you something, Gary."

"Yes?"

She sat down next to him, and put her arm around his shoulder. "I have accepted the fact that Yeshua is Messiah."

Gary searched his wife's face for any signs of uncertainty. He was skeptical of her confession. Shirley was always believing in something new. It usually depended on what book she had recently read, or what seminar she had last attended or, in the case of the Mellers, what people she'd recently come to know. Often, she took different parts from each persuasion and melded them together, to fit her specific needs.

Gary didn't really believe this latest "revelation" would last any longer than had any of her other beliefs in various spiritual philosophies. He was certain this one would be just as short-lived.

"What has caused you to change your opinion?" he asked carefully, trying to gauge whether or not this time her words had any more depth than the others.

"Freda explained to me how her life has been transformed. I was so gripped by her sincerity and love of God that I wanted what she had. I felt it, it emanates from her. I asked how I could get it. All I had to do, she said, was to pray to God through Yeshua, Jesus, and ask him to forgive me of all my sins. That's all, Gary."

He tried not to let his deepening skepticism show on his face.

"Well?" His voice was studiously even.

"I did that. She then said I should begin reading the Hebrew Scriptures and the New Testament—the *Brit Hadashah*—to gain understanding of what it all means to *my* life."

Shirley's words were full of a vibrancy Gary had never heard from her before. Her eyes shone. She had a peaceful, serene smile. It was comfortingly beautiful.

Though Gary noted these specific, outward changes, he still remained unmoved in his own mind. He just didn't feel what she felt, yet he didn't have the heart to tell his wife this. He was certain these new ideas of hers would prove as fleeting as her last belief. Experience had taught him that the less he questioned her sincerity, the shorter the time she spent telling him about her newest idea.

Here she goes again, he said to himself, thinking Shirley felt that this Yeshua was the latest means of liberation from her heavy emotional burdens, just as she had propounded other paths to peace.

What made this different from the rest?

Gary figured that this was just another spiritual bandage with which to wrap Shirley's emotional wounds.

Since reaching young adulthood, he had invested a great deal of time and effort into rekindling his awareness of his Jewish roots and immersing himself in the study of traditional, time-honored Judaism. Though Gary admitted that he presently didn't practice his faith as he had in the past, the apparent, inherent differences between Judaism and this Jesus and his Christianity were reason enough to reject him. Jesus—or, in Hebrew, Yeshua as Shirley was now calling him—simply had no direct relevance to his life. Belief in him was contrary to every belief and understanding he had ever learned as a Jew.

As the days went by, Shirley seemed to grow more serene and certain. Even in the face of her husband's skepticism, not once did she waver in her dedication to the one whom she called "Yeshua."

While Shirley became stronger in her spiritual certainty, her mentor, Freda gently continued to offer input into Gary's belief system.

In turn, he built a hard wall against both of them, determined not to listen further to anything more about this supposed Messiah. He certainly was not interested in hearing any more of Freda's lectures, nor in witnessing Shirley's never-ending exuberance.

One day, when Freda offered Gary a cassette tape and encouraged him to listen, he began to lose the tenuous grip he was holding on his temper and good manners. He was getting this story from his wife, on a daily basis, and here was Freda, *again*, trying to "make" him change his mind.

He looked at her and took a deep breath. "I don't want to be rude," he began, carefully trying to keep his voice very even, "but..."

"Take it," she softly interrupted. "Play it when you have the chance. What can it hurt to listen? You don't have to agree."

Gary didn't want to become combative, but neither did he want any part of Freda's tape or her well-intentioned concerns. He began to tick off a long list of every atrocity he could recall that had ever been done to Jews over the centuries in the name of Jesus and Christianity.

She nodded. She understood. Her gentle smile told him that she had expected the words even before he had said them. She seemed to be prepared for his refusal to listen. However, she was just as solidly determined to make her point. She shoved the tape into Gary's hand, forcing his fingers, one by one, around the plastic case.

"Listen to it, Gary."

Short of becoming outright confrontational, he felt he had no other choice but reluctantly to accept the tape. Slipping it carelessly into his pocket, he quickly forgot about it.

One Sunday morning, about a week later, Gary prepared to take a bath. Climbing into the tub, his leg reaching over the edge into the water, he found himself suddenly remembering Freda's tape. The thought came to him unbidden. At first he rejected it, and continued into the hot bath water.

However, he couldn't let go of the idea and curiosity got the better of him. Standing half-in and half-out of the tub, he made a quick decision and moved to retrieve the tape from his coat pocket. It wouldn't hurt to listen.

Returning to the bathroom, finally soaking in steamy, soapy water, he listened to the words of Jan Willem Van der Hoeven, a Dutch man living in Jerusalem. The introduction stated that Van der Hoeven was the co-founder of the International Christian Embassy of Jerusalem. He was addressing a gathering of gentile Christians. Gary couldn't deny that the lecture was a powerful delivery on Christianity's role in anti-semitism and the church's apathy during the Holocaust. It minced no words and allowed no excuses.

What really affected Gary, his bath nearly forgotten as the water chilled around him, was how Van der Hoeven spoke passionately of Yeshua, the Jew. He pointedly stated that Yeshua was born and raised a Jew, died a Jew, and would return to Israel and the world as a Jew. Yeshua had been a man of intense suffering who, through his extensive trials and humiliations on earth, had never lost sight of his desire to see peace and love prevail.

At that exact moment, everything fell into place for Gary. It dawned on him, with a realization that at first was fully intellectual, that this Yeshua, this *Jew*, was the Messiah, the one spoken of by Daniel in the ninth chapter of the *Tenach*. Yeshua was the Jewish Messiah! How positively amazing!

Gary now saw it as obvious, a truth he had always known, as if it was an axiom he had known since grade school. Yeshua was indeed a Jew who lived as a Jew and loved the Torah. Yeshua was sent by God to save a hurting world.

Shaking his head, he realized where he was, and knew that he'd been in the tub quite some time. Shirley would soon wonder what had happened to him. He quickly emerged from the tub, exited the bathroom and went looking for his wife.

"Love, I understand," he told her as she sat doing her needlepoint.

"What, Gary?" She looked up at him, smiling. "What do you understand?"

"I finally understand that Yeshua is the Jewish Messiah, the promised one."

□□□

The first people Gary and Shirley wanted to share their joint belief with were Don and Freda. Enthusiastically, they invited the couple to their house that evening for drinks and discussion.

"Bring your bathing suits and join us in the jacuzzi!"

After giving an animated recitation of how they'd each separately come to the realization of Yeshua as the Messiah, Gary looked back and forth from Don to Freda and asked eagerly, "What happens next? What are we to do now?"

"You need to learn more about Yeshua. This is only the beginning. It'll grow more exciting every day."

"How do we learn more?" Shirley persisted.

Freda and Don suggested Gary and Shirley begin by attending a Bible study; they had to learn to trust in the Lord daily and try to understand God's revelations to his people about his son, the Messiah. Freda and Don belonged to a church in Harare, and invited Gary and Shirley to visit on Sunday. Bible studies and countless learning experiences would certainly follow.

The Mellers began to instruct the Beresfords on how to begin their spiritual journey with the Messiah. Gary and Shirley were eager, hungering for that instruction. It was a lovely evening in Harare—the air was warm and comfortable, and a breeze had just come up as the sun began to set. The weather was perfect for sharing the simple comforts of friendship.

The two couples praised the Lord for such an abundant, glorious lifestyle and leaned back. Enjoying the moment, they could only believe that to know Yeshua and learn more about him would mean worldly security, a comfortable existence, and continued life after their earthly death. Their elemental understanding had only just begun.

On Sunday, both Gary and Shirley were nervous at the idea of attending a church. Though this wasn't the first time for them, they'd never found being in a gentile house of God to be any kind of a spiritual experience with which they connected.

Before they had gone as skeptics. This time they would enter as believers, *Jewish* believers. They would be welcomed into a church, a Christian house of God. This was a place where Jesus was expected to speak to anyone who would listen. They wanted to listen, though they had no idea what to expect.

Upon entering with Don and Freda, the Beresfords were greeted warmly by church members. People talked animatedly to each other and to them, laughing, often offering a hug or a pat on the back. There was a tangible, sincere love which permeated this group. Still, something wasn't right. As Gary sat in the pew, Shirley was ramrod straight next to him with her hands fidgeting in her lap. He carefully observed the church service as it unfolded: the movements of the congregants in each part of the service, the musical selections of the band, the pastor's passionate address replete with Christian terminology foreign to a Jew's ears. Gary felt guilty. Alienated. Out of his element. As if he'd walked in on a friendly, foreign family celebration. Despite the presence of God so evident everywhere around him, he felt removed from the experience.

He recalled the other times he'd been in a church. As a young boy of eight, he had entered a Methodist house of worship for a funeral, wondering why no one had their head covered like they did in synagogue. As a teenager he accompanied his Catholic girlfriend to Mass on Easter Sunday, confused as he heard the priest passionately proclaim that Christ had died at the hands of the Jews.

This was different. Wasn't it? He and Shirley now believed in

Yeshua and had come to worship among like-minded people. Then why did Gary continue to sense that this wasn't a place for him? No longer that Jewish boy condemned for the death of a man he had never known; yet, in his heart, he did not perceive this place as one in which he belonged.

Though they both felt uncomfortable with the worship format and sensed that the church atmosphere would forever be alien to them, Gary and Shirley couldn't bear to lose the spiritual connection they'd just found. They had nowhere else to go. They admitted to each other that they *were* learning about Yeshua through the church. The pastor, Gary Strong, was a deeply spiritual, kindhearted man who taught God's Word well.

Lost in the growing confusion of being thrust into a new situation where they felt nearly alone, Gary and Shirley weighed their options. Decidedly their options were few indeed. For the time being, they decided to look upon church as a learning experience, vital in their new lives as believers. Although Freda and Don were Jews, like themselves, they didn't seem to feel the same sense of separation which the Beresfords felt.

Gary and Shirley knew of no other Jewish believers to whom they might turn for guidance. They continued to attend church with the Mellers until they could find a more Jewish atmosphere in which to learn about Yeshua—if such a place existed. The church was, they reasoned, a house of God, even if they weren't accustomed to its ways.

□ □ □

It wasn't long after their first few meetings at the church that the Jewish organization to which Gary and Don belonged, the Hebrew Order of David, discovered their new religious convictions. Both men were called, without prior notice, before the executive committee and bluntly asked why they had rejected their Jewish identity.

"I have not rejected my Jewish identity," Gary replied with determination. Don's turn to face the interrogation was yet to come.

"You *do* claim now to believe in Jesus, do you not?"

"Yes, I do," Gary answered.

"And you don't see that as a rejection of Judaism?"

"No."

"How can you possibly reconcile the two?"

Gary thought hard before answering their question. It was clear that this was a valuable opportunity, not merely to defend himself, but to clarify the confusion that surrounded his faith.

"Jesus was a Jew, was he not?" Gary spoke politely, yet with conviction.

Soon the discussion became more and more confrontational. Don was also forced to defend his position. Before long, it became obvious that this exchange was becoming unfruitful. Both men strongly affirmed their beliefs while carefully answering the battery of questions from the committee. In spite of their rhetoric and resolve, Gary and Don were instructed that, if they would not renounce their belief in Yeshua, they would be forced to resign from the Order.

Gary exclaimed, "I don't think that's right!"

"I'm sorry," was the unfeeling answer. "This is how it has to be."

"What are we doing wrong?" Gary persisted. "Prove to me that Don and I have renounced our Jewish identity. I'll resign if you can do that. Otherwise, I will not."

Gary finally, and unhappily, accepted the facts—this discussion was going nowhere; the committee would not give in, and he and Don were unceremoniously ostracized.

Gary recognized that the mental jousting had been detrimental to their efforts; the committee was immovable and even more hostile than before. Nevertheless, he would not agree to the committee's terms. Holding fast to his new beliefs, he left the meeting with his refusal to resign hanging between him and the Order.

This effectively put him at odds with the entire Jewish community he and Shirley had eagerly embraced.

Anger seethed within him and he left the room without a backward glance. How could anyone *dare* to tell him he was no longer a Jew? What right did they have to say such a thing?!

Gary and Shirley continued to interact with the local Jewish crowd over the following weeks. They shared Shabbat—Sabbath—meals, attended synagogue, and frequented the predominantly Jewish country club. However, people that they had previously called their friends now looked at them askance. Discussion of issues of importance to the Hebrew Order and the community at large were cautiously avoided in front of them. People whispered as they walked by.

The Beresfords sensed that their lifestyle was about to change drastically. The Hebrew Order of David finally overrode Gary's refusal to resign by forcibly and officially kicking him out. He was told never to return as long as he and his wife continued to believe in Yeshua as the Messiah. Don suffered the same fate.

As far as the Hebrew Order and the community "in-crowd" were concerned, Gary and Shirley Beresford had become traitors to all that being Jewish stood for. Gary and Shirley knew, deep inside them, that this would be only the first of many estrangements they would experience.

Their commitment to Yeshua had seemed simple, so right to them. It had offered inner peace to Shirley. It was so logical to Gary. It made perfect sense. Yeshua was a Jew. Why couldn't their Jewish brothers and sisters see this obvious fact? *They* had seen it. Why was it so difficult for *others* to understand?

Chapter Seven
THE AWAKENING

It was late 1985 and Gary and Shirley grew steadily in their spiritual and intellectual belief in Yeshua the Messiah. They continued to feel the overwhelming joy a young child feels when making a new friend, getting to know that friend, sharing and loving together. It was a day-to-day discovery for them, one they not only welcomed, but encouraged.

They had read through the Scriptures before, but at those times their look into the Book had been superficial. Then they had been unbelievers. Now they felt compelled to take a fresh view of what God was saying to them and what he wanted specifically for their lives.

Delving into the Scriptures as a couple, starting at Genesis and working through the entirety, including the New Testament, they prayed that God would teach them both separately and together what he wanted them to know about the Messiah. They also desired to learn how to apply his words as practical truths to their everyday lives.

As they shared with one another specific passages that touched them, one pointed message made itself known to Gary over and over. The Scripture was filled with references to the return of God's chosen people to the land of Israel. The more he reflected on these passages, the more they jumped out at him, as if forcing him to pay attention. He became convinced it was God's definite will that the Jews, as a people, return to live and worship in the promised land.

In the Old Testament, Gary read Ezekiel's message from God, "For I will take you from the nations, gather you from all the lands, and bring you into your own land." The certainty of this promise shimmered on the page before him. Chills of excitement went through him as he read the prophecy of Amos, "I will also plant them on their land, and they will not again be rooted out from their land which I have given them."

Jews should be in Israel. This was biblical fact. Ultimately, all Jews were meant to live in the promised land. It was becoming clear to Gary that Israel was, indeed, that promised land, a place God had given centuries ago as a special haven for the Jewish people.

In this new understanding, Gary began to feel an insistent hope, a budding seed of belief opening up and growing inside him. The restoration of the Jewish people to Israel was to be the start of their spiritual rebirth as a people. Once they were restored, the Messiah Yeshua would return.

He flipped forward through the pages of the Bible to the words of Paul, in the eleventh chapter of his letter to the Romans ". . .all Israel will be saved; just as it is written, 'The deliverer will come from Zion, he will remove ungodliness from Jacob. And this is my covenant with them, when I take away their sins.'"

Gary clapped his hands together and laughed aloud. This was what he had waited for his whole life! Now he knew.

The more he and Shirley studied the Scriptures, on their own and together, the more certain Gary became that Israel not only figured into the intricate tapestry of future Jewish history, but that it was to be a part of his own future, as well. His future and Shirley's.

On a Monday morning, with the shower pounding on his head, he pondered, as he had been doing almost all his waking hours, what this might all ultimately mean to them personally. He wondered why it was that he could think of nothing else.

Standing directly under the showerhead, the water streamed onto Gary's face. His eyes were closed. The heat permeated the air around him and he suddenly felt an overwhelming presence swirling in the steam, seeping into his pores. As the water pounded his body, he leaned against the tiles on the wall and lost all realization of time and place.

He could sense his mind moving to another plane, a place where he became aware only of God. He felt, saw, smelled, sensed, even touched only the presence of God. All other realities ceased to exist for that moment. It was as if God were right there with him.

He "saw" Israel as if he were flying over it. The physical country, the people as they went about their day. An outline of God's encompassing plan for the country and the people overtook his mind. He knew that he was being told to go to Israel. The Lord had work for him to do there.

He had no choice. He knew there was nothing else for him to do, no room for argument or even discussion. His future lay in Israel from this day forward, not in simply thinking about it or in repeated intellectual talk. God wanted Gary Beresford physically in Israel.

□ □ □

"What are you doing, Gary?"

He stood there dripping, a towel around his waist. His hair

uncombed. His arms hung at his side. He was standing in the middle of his bedroom with no idea as to when he'd gotten there or how long he'd been in the shower before he came into the room.

The ramifications of what he knew he must do now ran rampant through his mind. Dizzy, he was sure he must look a wild sight to Shirley. He also knew the directive he had accepted would come as a big blow to her.

He remembered that Shirley did not like Israel.

Gary had to ignore that. He just couldn't deal with it at this point. With no subtlety or warning, he blurted out, "Sweetheart, we're moving to Israel. God wants us to live there. He spoke to me in the shower. I know this is the right thing for us to do. We don't have a choice."

She stared at him. Her eyes were huge; her expression blank. Her mouth was open, yet words would not come. Her face seemed to say that he was beyond help and ready for the insane asylum.

Gary briefly considered her expressed hatred of the country and her determination never again to set foot in Israel. It was certainly no surprise to him when his words brought a dumbfounded reaction from his wife. How was he going to convince her to change her mind?

"But Gary...."

"I've got to go to work right now. We'll discuss this later this evening." He had given her no time to consider her doubts. Nor had he told her all that God had revealed to him regarding their call in Israel, or the future of Jews as a whole.

It seemed best to leave the situation in God's hands. Gary threw on his clothes, gave Shirley a quick kiss, and rushed out the door and to the office. He was leaving his wife in a veritable state of shock but there was nothing else he could think to do.

□□□

Gary was aware of an Israeli law called the Law of Return, one of the first bills passed in the State of Israel in 1950, soon after the country had achieved independence. The law established the ancient Jewish hope as a national policy; never again would any Jew be denied a homeland. This edict authorized Jews from all over the world to become citizens of the Jewish state, virtually upon arrival.

The first part of the law stated, "Every Jew is entitled to enter Israel as an *oleh*" (a Jew immigrating to Israel). All it required was the determination that the emigré was, indeed, Jewish. The second part, as amended in 1970, read, "For the purposes [of this law]...a Jew is a person born to a Jewish mother or converted to Judaism, and who is not a member of another faith."

Gary pondered the requirements. He and Shirley certainly fit the criteria. That evening over dinner, Gary cautiously asked her if she had given any further consideration to his earlier declaration. He would use the Law of Return to legally secure their eventual physical immigration; yet, right now, he was relying on God to help his wife understand why that immigration was right for them.

"I've not given in to my personal feelings," she replied cautiously, not looking in his eyes, "so that I can try and seek God's will on this. I will give the idea a chance." Her glance came up, catching his. "I promise."

Gary knew he could ask no more and he grabbed her hand and squeezed it, smiling. At least Shirley had allowed for the possibility that God did want them in Israel. He was certain that she would ultimately do what the Lord wanted.

Later that night he encouraged her to join him in taking an in-depth look into how the Scriptures pertained to the Jew's return as a people to Israel. This proved to be an extended search. As the lamp next to them burned well into the early morning hours, the two found hundreds of relevant passages. The plethora of Bible references convinced Shirley, as Gary had been, that, sooner or later, it was God's will to have his chosen people, the Jews, return to Israel.

Yet was it truly his will to specifically send Shirley and Gary to Israel, now, to live for the rest of their lives?

This question had not been answered in her mind. Still, Shirley acknowledged that Scripture showed Israel to be the land promised to the Jewish people as a whole. She agreed that the next step would be to re-experience it themselves. Another visit was in order. She needed to see the country again to decide if she would react as she had on her first visit. Maybe the Lord would change her mind.

Gary firmly believed God would speak to his wife as he had spoken to him. At least Shirley was open to the possibilities now. For that Gary was truly grateful.

□□□

Zimbabwe had no diplomatic relations with Israel and had, in fact, become extremely antagonistic towards the Jewish state. With this in mind, the Beresfords booked a flight through Rome to Tel Aviv. Pro-Israeli friends in Zimbabwe made arrangements for them to stay in a small apartment with a tiny kitchen and air-conditioning. Upon arrival in the land, they found their accommodations adequate.

The view from the apartment, however, was much more than adequate, even to Shirley's skeptical eyes. The apartment building overlooked Ben Yehuda mall in downtown Jerusalem, offering a panorama as far as they could see. They viewed the cosmopolitan atmosphere of the modern city against the backdrop of the historical sights of the biblical land of Israel.

Early that evening, as the sun made a magnificent show of setting, they stood on the rooftop, their arms around each other, and surveyed everything below. The breeze whipped at the tendrils of Shirley's hair and, with a gentle smile, Gary put the wisps back into place.

There was a spark of home to the scene. Somehow it felt right.

□□□

The next day they spent time with Gary's cousin from England, John, and his family. John had immigrated to Israel twelve years before, after marrying the daughter of an English rabbi; now they had three young daughters of their own. The family was well-integrated into Israeli society and lived a satisfying, Orthodox Jewish life.

It had been eighteen years since Gary had last seen John in England, and everything was drastically different. Now, in Israel, they rekindled their familial relationship amidst the unique, ancient atmosphere, and talked for many hours about the Beresfords' possible move to Israel.

As John and his family related their personal experiences, Gary and Shirley began to talk with an excitement about Israel that they had not shared together until that moment. Gary was thrilled as his wife seemed to look positively towards a chance to live here. Her acceptance was growing in small increments—a joy to observe as it unfolded.

They listened intently to John's stories of contentment despite the hardships of adapting to a very different lifestyle. They were comforted by the idea that they would have English-speaking family of the same age in close proximity if, indeed, they decided to make the move.

Next, they were off for a tour around Jerusalem, their first priority being a visit to the Ministry of Absorption. The office was in an area dotted with high-rise government buildings near the Knesset, Israel's Parliament.

A security guard approached them and Gary asked to be directed to where they might learn about the process of immigration. The guard didn't understand his broken Hebrew. Gary tried again. After several minutes of halting, frustrating communications, Gary finally understood that they were being asked to present personal identification.

He fished through his pockets for his passport. Shirley looked in her purse. With a sinking feeling, they realized they'd left both passports at their apartment. Reaching back into his pocket, never taking his eyes off his wife, Gary yanked out the first item his fingers made contact with—a Hertz Rent-a-Car card.

The guard looked at it, his expression blank. Then he glanced up at Gary and Shirley with a puzzled frown, then looked back down at the card. With an impatient flourish, he waved them off to an office down the corridor from where they stood.

"He doesn't read English," Gary whispered, barely suppressing a chuckle.

Finally in the immigration office, Gary approached the reception desk. "We wish to make *aliyah*, to immigrate, and need to know about the different areas that would be good to settle in. We'd also like to know about the *kibbutzim* available."

"I'm sorry, sir. You and your wife are too old to be considered for membership on a *kibbutz*." (A *kibbutz* is a communal settlement.)

Gary and Shirley glanced at each other with raised eyebrows. It was difficult to hide the amusement tickling the corners of their mouths. They weren't aware that they were *old*.

"However..." the young woman went on patiently to offer valuable information on different areas of the country, telling them of the *Tour V'aleh* offices, which dealt specifically with prospective immigrants seeking details about the areas. Gary and Shirley took in all that they heard, thanked the receptionist for her time, and left the building.

Already early afternoon, they hadn't begun their tour of the city. The heat was sweltering and they were hungry. They arrived at the Jaffa Gate entrance to the Old City of Jerusalem and stopped for a snack. From there, they wended their way through the Arab market—dividing the Christian Quarter on the left from the Armenian and Jewish Quarters on the right.

The ancient, narrow, stone passageway bustled with tourists moving from vendor to vendor. The air was steeped with the pungent, lingering aroma of Middle Eastern spices. Piercing cries of merchants enticing shoppers to purchase their goods could be heard everywhere. An unrelenting strain of Arab music assaulted their unaccustomed ears. In the midst of all this Israeli life, armed soldiers walked with familiarity amongst the crowd. This, too, was part of the accepted scenery.

Gary and Shirley headed for the Western Wall, the focal point for Jewish prayer. Trees framed the area. Entering the plaza faced with Jerusalem stone, they prepared themselves to hear God's voice. They were confident that he would speak directly to them.

The couple walked hand-in-hand down the broad steps which led to the prayer areas, gave each other a comforting smile, and parted. Gary, briefly recalling his visit to this very location as a young teenager with his dad, headed left, towards the men's section. Shirley, tying on a scarf over her head, approached the women's entrance.

This day she would hear the Lord. He would tell her how to proceed. Should she and Gary move to Israel, make yet another new life in a land that had previously seemed so foreign and uninviting to her? They had already made so many moves, both separately and together; this one would be monumental.

Or should they stay in Zimbabwe for now, eventually settling in England as they had originally planned? This prayer time was crucial; it would decide their future.

She pressed her head against the ancient stones and asked for God's wisdom and guidance. Scraps of paper had, here and there, been slipped in the cracks, requests from others for God's attention. She didn't pay them much notice. The continuous, low-pitched drone of people praying became a comforting backdrop for the jumbled thoughts going through her overfilled brain.

Determined and single-minded, Shirley leaned against the stones. All sense of the present was lost. Time and space ceased to exist, to be replaced by the deep, abiding, secure presence of God, even sturdier than the ancient wall. There was nothing but God.

Shirley's body relaxed completely, suddenly filled with a sensation of peace.

And as in many of her prayer times, she realized that the Lord wanted her to know he would give her a definite answer in his time, not hers. She must have patience. He was with her, and with Gary. That was all she needed to know right now.

She rejoined her husband and spoke of the tranquility that had enveloped her. She had found serenity and would hold on to it no matter what their future. She would stop trying to second-guess him; instead, she would await his direction, and follow it without question.

Wanting to find a quiet place, away from the crowds, to reflect without interruption on each of the morning's events, Gary and Shirley headed for the Garden Tomb. Passing through the gate, they glanced around, marveling at the beauty and significance of where they were and why they were there. They were at peace. They were where they were meant to be.

They located a bench facing the tomb and sat, without speaking, soaking up the serenity around them. After a while, a group of tourists arrived and sat near them. A bearded man stood, faced the people, and softly began to explain the spiritual and historical significance of the spot.

He spoke about the Messiah, about the short but intense life on earth of this gentle man called Yeshua, and how this very site might well be where Messiah Yeshua's burial chamber was located. He then took *matzah*, unleavened bread, and a bottle of red grape juice from a pouch he carried at his side and asked, looking all around him, "Are there any Jewish men present?"

Gary glanced up. "I am Jewish." His voice was low, subdued by this bearded stranger's powerfully-touching words.

The man came over and extended his hand in greeting. "Shalom! I'm Zola Levitt, a Jewish believer in Yeshua from Dallas, Texas. I am here to lead a tour for these believers. This is their first visit to the Holy Land."

Gary stood, introducing himself as he shook the man's hand.

Mr. Levitt asked, "Would you be willing to offer the Jewish blessing of thanks over this fruit of the vine, the ancient blessing which Yeshua would have recited shortly before his death?"

Gary felt as if the Lord's smile, bestowed upon them through an already-eventful day, continued to shine down through this stranger's request. He gratefully accepted the honor and they all shared the sanctity of the moment.

Later, back in their small apartment, Gary and Shirley talked long into the first hours of the next morning about what had happened to them in one short day. They cuddled, laughed, and thanked God for what he had already shown them. The Lord was walking with them every step of their way, guiding and introducing them to a side of Israel neither had realized existed. Israel wasn't in any way as either had expected or as they had previously experienced.

□□□

It was early the next day; the heat had not yet climbed to its peak. Gary and Shirley headed down the Jerusalem-Tel Aviv highway to *Moshav Yad HaShomnah*, a community founded by Finnish Christians, located eight miles from Jerusalem, in the Judean Hills. They were accompanying newfound Messianic Jewish friends to a gathering of believers for *Shavuot*—the Feast of Weeks, Pentecost.

Exiting the car and walking up a hill towards a very large log cabin, they were surprised to discover a huge crowd on the other side. A group of six musicians were playing Israeli songs. The music had just begun. Many in the crowd joined in the singing, while others danced.

There was great diversity among the people present. Some were dressed casually in shorts and tee shirts, while others wore Orthodox Jewish garb. Several wore scull caps and ritual fringes, and some even had *peyot*, sidecurls. Gary and Shirley learned that gentiles were interspersed among the Jews. This amazed and delighted them.

It was a sight previously unseen by the Beresfords. Encouraged and reassured to see men and women, boys and girls, young and old, expressing their Jewish identity in relation to a solid belief in Yeshua as the Messiah, they sensed how very different and refreshing this was from their first encounter with believers at the church in Zimbabwe.

Gary finally experienced the sense of acceptance and completion that he had been missing. It draped itself over him like a comforting, warm cloak. He and Shirley were finally where they belonged. This was what the Lord wanted for them.

After a delicious and filling lunch, Shirley wanted to be alone. She walked off to an isolated spot next to a large boulder, feeling that God finally had instructions for her, and that this would be the time and the place where he would reveal them. With a sense of expectancy, she told Gary she had to go out alone for awhile, excused herself, and moved far away from the crowd. She waited. And she prayed.

□□□

Shirley had been gone over an hour. Glancing away from the group of people with whom he was talking, Gary saw his wife slowly coming towards him. On her face was a look of great relief. Her features shone with a joy he had seen before only when she was in spiritual communion with her Lord. He walked away from the others and went to her, taking her hand.

"He spoke to me, Gary," she breathed, looking up at him, her smile wide. "It *is* his will for us to move to Israel."

Chapter Eight

YOU ARE NOT A JEW

Back in Zimbabwe, Gary and Shirley set about the determined task of selling their home and preparing for their move to Israel. The most difficult part for Gary would be explaining their decision to his parents. He knew it would be hard, if not impossible, for them to accept the idea that he was leaving. His father's health was forever in question and, in Zimbabwe, they lived only ten minutes away. Their close proximity was a comfort to his parents in their advancing years.

Now he was forced to tell them he was moving four-and-one-half thousand miles away.

It had become Gary and Shirley's common practice now to pray before making any decision that would significantly impact their lives. After seeking the Lord's presence and asking for his perfect guidance, Gary felt his determination reinforced. Arranging a brunch with his parents the Sunday after their return from Israel, the couple contemplated their approach.

The four of them sat comfortably around the elder Beresfords' table, enjoying, as always, a delicious, well-cooked meal. Conversation was general and varied, not immediately related to Gary and Shirley's news.

Finally, Gary collected his nerve and cleared his throat. "We are planning to move to Israel."

No response. A thick, uncomfortable silence ensued which Gary feared would last forever. Finally his parents reacted, their emotions brimming over their faces. His mother cried, "Do you know what you're doing? Do you really understand? What do you plan to do to make a living?"

"We—"

"Gary," his father interrupted, not looking at his wife, "why this sudden desire? Whatever brought this on?"

"It's not sudden," Shirley explained quietly, with conviction. "The Lord has been impressing this upon us for several months. I, too, was skeptical until our recent visit to Israel, but now I know. This is the right thing for us. It is." She went on, trying to explain about God's plan and that they had learned that it was his purpose to restore the Jewish population to the land of Israel.

"Please listen." Gary implored his parents, looking from one to the other, asking them with his eyes as well as his words to understand. "The negative attitude towards Israel now growing within the Zimbabwean government indicates that the future of Jews in this country is uncertain at best. Haven't you seen how the state colors television and radio against us, inciting the public to look down on Israel? What can the future hold for Jews here, in this country?!"

Gary took a deep, steadying breath. "It's true, we don't yet have any focused idea of how we'll make our living there, or exactly where we'll live. But these answers will be provided in God's time. I know you can't understand how we can make such a move based on faith alone. Nevertheless, it *is* the right decision for us. We're both very sure."

His words didn't make the impression for which he had prayed. His parents' sad features revealed their resignation. They knew that he and Shirley had resolved to make this move, and that nothing they might say would change that decision. Their minds grasped the finality of the decision, but their hearts found accepting it extremely difficult. Their voices burdened with sadness, they would reluctantly watch their only son leave them, perhaps for good.

Disclosure now behind them but the pain fresh in their hearts, Gary and Shirley left his parents in a state of anguish. There was nothing else they could do.

Yet another set of confrontations awaited them. A visit to South Africa was needed. Their children had to be told.

□□□

At the airport in Johannesburg, Gary and Shirley were met by Shirley's daughter, Marlene. It was late in the evening and they were exhausted, so they retired, deciding to talk to her whole family the next day. Marlene already knew of and accepted their decision.

The family gathered for a barbecue at Shirley's sister's house. Calmly, Gary and Shirley revealed their intentions. Affirming their belief that the move was in accordance with God's call on their lives, they would trust him for all their needs. It was as simple, and as complex, as that. Details were important, but were not their initial priority.

The first words from one of Shirley's sons were, "You're going to *what?* No, no, That's foolish."

He continued, saying that the lifestyle in Israel would be too difficult. They wouldn't be able to adjust to such a foreign way of life.

Again, Gary and Shirley found themselves looking down the barrel of familial discontent and disagreement. Other members of their family offered their opinions. Concern, cautious encouragement, skepticism, downright disbelief—every sort of emotion popped out from those gathered.

Another of Shirley's sons, along with Marlene, felt that their mother had become a much stronger person in recent years; she and Gary would be fine, would even prosper, in Israel. They expressed their own interest in visiting them there once they were settled in, and talked about the idea of immigrating at some later date.

Gary and Shirley brimmed with certainty and made it clear that the family simply had to accept this move. They *would* immigrate to Israel. The meeting ended with that fact understood, if not accepted.

Last on the list of people to inform were Gary's two children. He rose the next morning, alone, and borrowed Marlene's car. His ex-wife was expecting him and, after exchanging brief, meaningless pleasantries with her, he took the children out to spend the entire day with them.

□ □ □

Joel was now nine years old, Lauren was six. Gary had looked forward to the opportunity to have this precious time with them; such outings had been rare in recent years. They started their day at an ice cream parlor; they talked about schoolwork, sports, hobbies, and friends. Lauren was studying ballet. Joel was an avid soccer player and enthusiast, like his father and grandfather before him.

It was winter and they couldn't visit outdoors, so Gary took the children to the mall to play miniature golf. The sound of their voices and laughter filled him with bittersweet pleasure; as the moments of their time together grew shorter, he knew he had to talk to them about his leaving. Trouble was, he didn't know where to begin. How to explain to his two young children that Daddy would be going far, far away and would live there, probably forever.

After lunch, Gary eyed his only workable chance. Riding around outlying neighborhoods, reminiscing through areas he had not seen since he had last lived in Johannesburg, he told them that he would be moving. Gary tried to make them understand why he was going, but he could tell from their blank expressions that they really didn't understand the full implications.

Their questions were simple, full of the curiosity of a child's mind. How long would Daddy be gone? Why did he have to go? Could they come live with him? Why not? How far away is 'far'? What was Israel like? Why did he have to go to still another country?

Joel and Lauren just could not seem to grasp the concept of great distances. After making his best attempt at an explanation, Gary finally returned them to their mother. Taking them in his arms for a long, tearful embrace, he sorrowfully let them go. He had to return to Shirley.

□□□

Monday morning in Johannesburg dawned chilly but clear. After a quick breakfast, Gary and Shirley drove with Marlene to her work and dropped her off. They took her car from there and made their way to the South African Zionist Federation building, where they were required to go to file for permission to immigrate.

They cleared security. Alighting from the elevator at the floor where immigration was handled, they were greeted by a comforting message emblazoned on the long corridor wall, "Welcome to Israel."

"We're getting there, love," Gary said, smiling and squeezing his wife's hand.

They entered the office. The receptionist, upon hearing the couple's request, reported that someone would be with them shortly. Officials of the Federation were appointed to the Agency to aid prospective immigrants. Gary and Shirley sat down to wait for one of these officials in the barren, lifeless office, whispering nervously with one another.

Within fifteen minutes, they were approached by a man, identifying himself as Skip Treisman. Gary and Shirley followed him into a cubbyhole of an office, explaining that they now lived in Zimbabwe though they were South African by birth, and wanted to apply for citizenship in Israel. They were given the appropriate forms to fill out and asked to exhibit their *ketubah*, the Jewish marriage certificate.

"I see no reason for any delay here, Mr. and Mrs. Beresford," Mr. Treisman informed them with a friendly, open smile at the end of their meeting. "The paperwork is, of course, nothing more than a formality. I'll contact you within the month with the details of your move."

He went on to advise them of how he might help them locate an apartment once they arrived in Israel, in Rishon L'tzion, a town just south of Tel Aviv. The Federation had an arrangement with the municipality of that city which worked with them in settling South African immigrants.

After listening to Mr. Treisman, Gary and Shirley felt they were all but moved to Israel. They held hands tightly as they left the immigration office, dreamily discussing what they would do first when they arrived in their new country. Gary leaned over and kissed his wife as they climbed into the car and headed back to Marlene's. They were ready to take on the task of preparing to move to Israel.

□ □ □

On the flight back to Zimbabwe, talk centered around everything they would have to do for their move. A hectic, daunting task, it was one they both eagerly welcomed. They needed to sell their house, dispose of any excess furniture, and make arrangements to pack carefully their collection of porcelain figurines.

Several real estate agents were contacted, and their property was evaluated. The market was buoyant due to the shortage of building materials which presently slowed down the construction of homes in Zimbabwe, and the cost of existing houses was on the rise. Their eight-room home was considered executive quality with its swimming pool, sauna, hot tub, and extensive, well-maintained grounds. There was also a small cottage to the back of the property where a gardener and housekeeper lived.

They both tendered resignations at their jobs, then proceeded to finish up existing workloads. They had allowed themselves a three-month organization period and would fiercely stick to that schedule. Three months to get everything done.

Shortly after their house was appraised, the Zimbabwean government hosted the Non-Aligned Countries Conference in Harare. An advertisement was put in the local papers for rental properties to house the heads of state attending the conference. The government offered payment in United States dollars, transferable to any other country in the world.

Gary immediately contacted the Zimbabwean government department in charge of this project and offered their home.

Within twenty-four hours an official knocked on their door, an impressive stack of forms under his arm. He politely surveyed their entire property, carefully noting everything he found. After an hour-and-a-half, he sat down with Gary and Shirley to discuss his findings.

Yes, he nodded resolutely as he looked through his paperwork, the Zimbabwean government would be pleased to hire their property for a period of six weeks.

Gary and Shirley thanked the official. After ushering him out the door at the end of the discussion, they embraced and thanked the Lord for intervening in such a marvelous, ingenious fashion. This latest development would provide them with enough money to make their initial transfer to Israel. They were proceeding smoothly and according to schedule.

□□□

Curiously, a month passed and not a single word had been heard from Mr. Treisman at the Federation. Gary called the office from work one morning to inquire as to the status of their immigration request.

"Mr. Treisman, this is Gary Beresford."

The official hesitated, clearing his voice but not speaking. The uncomfortable pause lengthened.

"Mr. Treisman," Gary started again, this time going right into his reason for calling, "my wife, Shirley, and I visited your office and submitted applications for Israeli citizenship. Have you any news for us? It has been a month."

Again, Treisman made nervous, unintelligible sounds before he finally replied, "Mr. Beresford, I've not received an answer from our Jerusalem office. Could you call me again next week? I promise to have an answer for you by then."

Gary heard the other man shuffling papers. Treisman hadn't said what he'd wanted to hear, but Gary shrugged, deciding they could wait one more week. He thanked Treisman for his help and hung up, still certain that things would soon be resolved. If this was the only glitch they encountered, they would still be in Israel in good time.

□□□

The following week passed rapidly amidst their continuing preparations. Little thought could be allotted for worries over delays and Gary and Shirley didn't feel any real need to be concerned. Paperwork was red tape. Red tape always took time.

When Gary once again had Treisman on the phone, he eagerly asked for a final response. When could they move?

"Uh, well, Mr. Beresford, I still don't have an answer for you."

Gary's stomach churned, sensing that something was dreadfully wrong. The realization hit him, hard and unexpected, as if a large truck had driven into his desk.

He'd had dealings years ago with the Zionist Federation and Youth Movement. He knew it never took more than four weeks to process immigrant applications. It just wasn't a lengthy process.

"I can't accept that, Mr. Treisman."

"I'm sorry, but that's the way it is."

"No," Gary replied with force, "that is *not* the way it is. There's more to this delay than you're telling me, and I want to know what's going on. Right now."

"It's very complicated."

"Now."

After much throat clearing and aborted efforts to put his words together, Treisman attempted to give a coherent answer. Almost apologetically, he said quietly, "Our office has been informed that, in the eyes of Israel, you and your wife are no longer Jews."

"What?!"

Treisman ignored Gary's loud interruption. "You are no longer Jews," he reiterated, "It seems as though you have converted to another religion."

"And what is this assumption based on?" Gary's voice was ice cold. He gripped the phone, trying to hold on to his rising temper.

I am no longer a Jew? he thought incredulously. *I am no longer a Jew?*

"You *are* members of the group, Jews for Jesus, aren't you?"

At first, Gary didn't trust himself to speak. Indignation and fury were so great that the effort to respond civilly tied up all ideas suddenly warring for attention in his head.

"Mr. Beresford? Are you?"

"No, Mr. Treisman, we are not." Gary's tone was strained, tight, and his words evenly spaced as if he were speaking to a difficult, addled child. "What exactly do you mean by 'converted to another religion'?" He ignored the group identity that had automatically been given to them. Most people seemed to immediately assume a

Jew who believed in the Messiah was part of an organization called Jews for Jesus.

"Converted. Belong to another religion. You understand the term, I'm sure."

"Listen well, sir. I am Jewish. My wife is Jewish. Our parents are Jewish. We are Jews, make no mistake about that. We *do* believe that Yeshua is the Messiah, but what has that to do with our being Jewish?"

"Sorry, but I can't help you, Mr. Beresford." Treisman sounded as if he were quickly tiring of this conversation. His discomfort had turned into aggravation. "We at the South African Zionist Federation office have been informed that you are no longer Jewish. Therefore, you are not eligible to become citizens of the State of Israel under the provisions of the Law of Return."

"This just cannot be," Gary persisted. "There must be a terrible misunderstanding. It is simply not true that we've stopped being Jewish. How can this situation be rectified?"

Treisman told Gary that there was little that he could—or would—do; however, if they were determined to pursue the matter, Gary should write a letter detailing everything he and Shirley believed, and send it to Treisman's attention at the Federation office. He would forward it on to Jerusalem.

Knowing he was up against an issue that couldn't be resolved at this level, Gary concluded the conversation and immediately dialed Shirley at her business. All thought of the work he still had left to do that day had been forgotten.

"Sweetheart, I have just gotten off the phone with Treisman. The news is not good."

"Tell me. What's happened?"

Gary sighed. He didn't want to break his wife's heart. "It seems that we are ineligible for citizenship."

"But why, Gary? Why? All Jews are eligible for citizenship in Israel."

"The Federation officials have declared that we are no longer

Jews because we believe that Yeshua is the Messiah. They say we have converted to another religion."

"No longer Jews? Who says so? Gary, God knows we are Jewish."

"But, love, it would seem that Federation officials have not consulted God in this matter. Treisman said the only hope we have is to draft a letter detailing our beliefs. If we send it in to him he will forward it to Jerusalem. He wasn't too promising."

They immediately prayed together there on the phone. They decided that Gary needed to immediately write and send the letter. Time was rapidly becoming their enemy.

After he hung up, Gary took a sheet of writing paper from his desk. Pen poised, he again prayed. "Lord," he asked aloud, "please guide my words as I compose this letter about our faith in you. I'm not sure what to say."

The two pages flowed out of him. First he gave the pedigree of their Jewish heritage, stating that they were born Jewish and would die Jewish. This, he avowed, was not negated when they accepted that Yeshua was the Jewish Messiah.

According to Jewish tradition, he continued, one who is born a Jew remains a Jew forever, regardless of his belief system. Being Jewish was a birthright, a heritage, unchangeable.

Shaking, Gary's hands folded the letter. Holding it a moment he sensed that this act would likely catapult him and Shirley into something which they didn't yet understand, but would consume the rest of their lives. With this letter, he sealed their fate. Somehow he knew this.

He dropped the letter in the mail slot. Now it was out of his hands.

□□□

"No. The answer is still, no."

Three weeks later Gary stood reading the response to their request for immigration. It had come directly from the World

Zionist Organization in Jerusalem. The letter that Treisman suggested Gary write had been handed up to the parent organization; now, he stared with disbelief at their cold, unyielding response.

"They will not issue us the necessary visas for citizenship in Israel. Shirley, they won't let us live there."

This came as a stunning blow. What a bitter irony. Now, after all these years, their lives were more Jewish than ever before.

So many people failed to understand what it meant to embrace and accept Yeshua, a Jew. Through Judaism, they had been drawn to Yeshua; and through Yeshua, they had found the way to become intimate with the Torah and the teachings that it contained. It was within their new belief that they had learned what it really meant to be Jewish.

They followed holidays, partook of daily prayer and study, and lived a distinctly Jewish lifestyle based on certain elements of *halakhah*, the Judaic system of walking according to God's law. For example, keeping a kosher house had become important to them, yet in Zimbabwe that had proven to be nearly impossible to do. The country lacked kosher foods. In moving to Israel, this facet of Jewish existence could easily be incorporated into their normal lifestyle and they looked forward to this.

Their heritage was now more precious to them. Before coming to faith in Yeshua, it had simply meant rules and regulations, practices they'd always been told were part of the package called "Judaism." They had followed these rules when and if it was convenient. They had ignored or discarded the practices which didn't suit them. Here, in the months since they had accepted Yeshua, being Jewish meant so much more than merely saying, "I'm Jewish."

Being a Jew was their identity, their very breath. Being a Jew was who and what they were. Practicing the Judaism of Yeshua was a privilege, something no longer to be avoided or interpreted; it was a lifestyle to be embraced.

Now, suddenly, someone—another Jew, no less—dared to tell them that in the sight of one of the worlds' largest Jewish organizations, in the sight of the country which they longed to be a part of, they were no longer Jews. What gave anyone the right to pass this kind of summary judgment on another person's heart or heritage? Could this truly be God's determination or was it, as it seemed, a mere declaration of man?

Would they accept the edict? *Could* they? Would they bow to the power and strength of those against them? Would they allow doubt to cloud their decision?

Or would they continue to uphold the ideal that God was directing them in this, even as they were aware that to fight would mean certain alienation from a way of life they'd always known? To fight, it would seem, also meant that they must strike out almost blindly. They would have to make their move with little knowledge of what awaited them upon their arrival in Israel.

Gary and Shirley prayed and talked, talked and prayed, worrying over how they should handle the turmoil into which they had been thrust. They didn't waver in their conviction that the Lord had shown them, surely and powerfully, in his Word, that their future was in Israel.

Yet that certainty was now sullied by the words of man. They found themselves doubting their own communications with God. Was he really speaking to them as individuals, or had they merely taken his words and confused them with their own wishes? Were they really meant to go to Israel *now*?

How could they be certain of the answers to these confusing questions?

In addition, they were overwhelmed by their natural feelings concerning the rejection that had been directed towards them by their own people. It was as if the entire world of Judaism had, in one letter, just tossed them away, thoughtlessly as pieces of garbage. Despite the comfort of friends who continued to rally around and support them, their sense of alienation was overpowering; they felt carelessly abandoned by their own Jewish people.

While the calendar ticked away precious days, Gary and Shirley agonized over how to proceed. If they went after Israeli citizenship, it would be useless to do so through the Zionist Federation. Now antagonistic towards the Beresfords, any more communications with them on this issue would be absolutely fruitless.

On the other hand, if they pursued immigration without enlisting the Federation's assistance, they had to trust solely and unequivocally in the Lord to provide for all their needs. Once again this called into play their wavering concern over whether or not God had in fact spoken to them and directed them to Israel at this specific time.

Gary and Shirley decided that they must forge on. After intensive prayer on both of their parts, they were once again certain they were doing the Lord's will. He did want them in Israel. And he wanted them to continue the fight to go to Israel now. Not sometime in the faraway future. Not at an unspecified, later date. This was something they must do, and continue to do, immediately. They would have to hold fast to the Lord for their needs.

They were painfully aware that their decision to immigrate to Israel would change their lives forever.

Chapter Nine

ON TO ISRAEL

Returning to their home once the Non-Aligned Nations Conference had ended, Gary and Shirley contacted various real estate agents to offer their house for final sale. It was a bittersweet task filled with countless opportunities to reminisce about times past, and to wonder over what lay ahead for them.

Their home was spacious, comfortable, beautifully decorated and fashionable, with more than enough room, even under generous standards. They had amassed a healthy fortune and tangible material possessions.

Their free time these days revolved around the pool, sauna, and various recreational facilities readily at their call both on their own grounds, as well as at the country club. Gary and Shirley had worked hard since their marriage to build a comfortable existence for themselves, and they had succeeded beyond their original expectations.

All of this easy living would be hard to give up, they knew, moving to a life of indecision, confusion, and unknown material resources. They realized they had come to a stage in their lives where physical comforts meant much to them and the lack of them would bring about certain stress.

One day, with the house on the market and as yet no buyer to be found, Shirley thought about these realities. Deep in her heart, Shirley still worried about abandoning the lifestyle which she so much enjoyed and to which she had become accustomed. She almost regretted agreeing to the move.

Shirley didn't share her uncertainties with anyone, not even her husband. One day, as she strolled casually through downtown Harare, Shirley walked past the storefronts, struggling with the thoughts that warred in her head. Here she had more—both materially and emotionally—than she'd ever had in her difficult life; here she felt more at ease. Yet now she was getting ready to leave it and start all over again. What was more, she would be moving to a life filled with nothing but unknowns. No home, no job, an unfamiliar culture.

Could this be the right move? Should they give it more thought? They had made a number of friends on their last visit to Israel, and a support network was in place to help ease their transition. In telling their story as guest speakers before various groups in Israel, they had met even more people who had offered ongoing assistance. Still, these were only strangers, and the whole idea was petrifying. It would be a complete change of lifestyle.

Looking in a store window, seeing her own confused and scared reflection staring sternly back at her, Shirley jumped at the startling sound of a powerful voice. It didn't come from behind her. It wasn't in front of her, nor was it beside her. The words were real, though, as the voice asked directly, forcefully, "If I were to return right now, what would you do with all your possessions?"

Cautiously, slowly, she looked around her. No one was anywhere near her. No one was even close enough to have spoken to her. Nonetheless the voice sounded so clear, right inside her head.

"What *would* you do?"

Shirley whirled around once again, then slumped against a nearby wall. She squeezed her eyes tightly shut. Was she now hearing imaginary voices? Was she going crazy?! She felt dizzy. What was happening to her?

Suddenly, the breathtaking realization broke upon her like a brand new smile. Of course. She knew who had spoken, and she was certain that not only had she definitely heard the words, but it had been no casual conversation with an uninvolved bystander.

The Lord was taking her to task, chiding her for her materialism and uncertainty. He was, in clear terms, letting Shirley know that to continue with such worldly, materialistic doubts would have a detrimental effect on her spiritual, marital, and, most likely, physical well-being.

She needed to find her security in the Lord, and only in him. He would have it no other way.

Returning the smile, she continued her walk. Now there were no doubts as to what she must do.

□□□

Less than a week later, a Jewish couple approached the Beresfords and, practically without negotiation, made a satisfactory offer on the house. They agreed to pay a small amount of the purchase price in South African "rands," allowing Gary and Shirley to buy a number of items while still in South Africa which they couldn't buy for export in Zimbabwe, things they knew they would need for their new home in Israel.

They hired an international moving company to pack their household goods and store them until they could be shipped to Israel via South Africa. With South Africa's economy in a downslide, and considering Zimbabwe's embrace of communism, it was evident that this country was becoming isolated from a free market system.

This fact created an unexpected problem for the Beresfords. They possessed a large amount of Zimbabwean dollars and needed to have them exchanged for hard currency. They applied to the Reserve Bank of Zimbabwe, but were told that they could not take one single penny out of the country. It was against the law.

The irony of their situation was almost laughable. Here, within Zimbabwe, they were considered quite wealthy, but elsewhere in the world they would be nothing more than paupers. As this weighed heavily on their minds, they bought up whatever valuable art items they knew for certain they could legally ship out of the country—paintings, figurines, sculpture—and prepared to have them packed for transit.

Gary and Shirley felt they had found a solution to their money problem. Despite the government's warnings to the contrary, they *could* take it with them.

□□□

The various purchases were made. There were now so many items to transport that, according to the movers, only a forty-foot container would suffice. Nothing smaller would do, yet no containers of this size were available.

They could acquire two twenty-footers without any rental problems, but it would involve extra paperwork and considerably higher costs. Their money was quickly being tied up elsewhere, and Gary and Shirley could not afford to put a single cent of it into extra shipping expenses.

Things were getting far too complicated. Gary phoned various shipping companies in a frantic search for a forty-foot container. He discovered that this was an unusual request for use in private transport. Any such containers that existed were already contracted by the Tobacco Marketing Board for governmental business.

That evening, Gary and Shirley prayed about the matter, knowing that something had to be decided upon very soon. Mentioning the situation to friends, they were surprised to receive a phone call the next morning. These same friends had been reading the newspaper over breakfast and noticed an advertisement for two forty-foot containers being sold, amazingly, for public transport.

Gary hung up the phone and immediately contacted the company. A man with a heavy accent told Gary that these shipping vessels were newly arrived from Germany. His company wished to dispose of them as quickly as they could. After asking a few more questions, Gary was comfortable that the containers were exactly what he needed. He'd take one, sight unseen, confident it would serve his purpose.

The German man, a bit mystified at the caller's eagerness, insisted Gary look before he purchased. Was he sure that he didn't want to inspect them first? Gary reassured him that wouldn't be necessary, and arranged to have the container collected and paid for the following day. He didn't need to inspect what God had provided!

With what remained of their money, Gary and Shirley purchased additional items that they were sure to need in Israel. Thinking that many products were either expensive or completely unobtainable in Israel, the Beresfords decided to ensure that they would not be lacking. Tea, coffee, toiletries, bed linen, and a large roll of wall-to-wall carpeting were added to possessions already prepared to leave the country.

As the time passed quickly, day-to-day life in Zimbabwe continued on its path of political unrest and national insecurity. Finances, politics, human rights, the difficulties mounted over these issues and many more, escalating into a growing, unease among the population. Watching and monitoring the news carefully, Gary and Shirley felt that they should accelerate their plans to leave.

Zimbabwe and South Africa were on the verge of closing their shared border due to unrest. If that border did close, Gary and Shirley knew they would be forced to use a transport route through Mozambique to the Port of Beira, and then on to Israel. Terrorist attacks and constant pilfering were two of many dangers on that route, and they hoped to sidestep such frightening possibilities.

Non-transferable money continued to be a concern. What was left had to be spent, but not wasted. Gary made certain to budget carefully to ensure that, by the time they left for Israel, their pockets would be virtually empty of Zimbabwean dollars.

To this end, they purchased two airline tickets for a brief trip to Victoria Falls and Kariba, a last vacation to the nicer parts of Zimbabwe. From there, they spent a week on the island of Mauritius in the Indian Ocean. Next, they bought two tickets to South Africa to give them the chance to see their families one more time before leaving the area for good. Afterwards, they would be on to Israel, their final destination.

Shirley went to South Africa ahead of Gary, who needed to make last minute preparations with the tax office in Harare. A clearance certificate was required to supplement their tax returns and, as he worked to get this secured, he realized that they just might be hit with a large tax bill. They had owned their house a fairly short time and had profited considerably by its sale. Tax-wise, this could prove to be a problem.

At about the same time, the shipping company informed him that an extra four thousand Zimbabwean dollars would be needed to cover the cost of shipping and packing. He no longer had enough extra money on hand for the added transport bill; in his scheme to ensure that there would be no money left over, he had disposed of virtually all of their cash. If the tax office told him he also owed money, in addition to what the shipping company now demanded, they would be in dire straits.

"Lord," he prayed aloud as he drove into the tax office parking lot, facing what was ahead of him with a shaky resolve, "please be good to us!" His hands squeezed the steering wheel with intensity.

He took a deep breath, and turned into a parking space.

A week later, when he returned to the office to collect his assessment, Gary was handed an innocent-looking slip of paper. No one beckoned him into their office; not a single person demanded that he wait to discuss the amount of money he owed the government.

Looking around, still waiting for someone to proffer the bad news, he glanced at the notice. Standing in the middle of the room, he continued to stare blankly at the paper in his hands, not really seeing what he read. The words simply didn't register. He went over it slowly a second time and finally realized what it meant. He understood what he had done, and the implications regarding his tax status.

Having over-assessed his personal funds, Gary was entitled—entitled!—to a full refund of exactly four thousand, nine hundred and fifty dollars. A refund! Not only did he not owe the government anything in taxes; *they* were going to pay *him*. Providentially, the amount enabled him to fulfill his obligations to the transport company and have a little left over.

□□□

When Gary finally made it to South Africa, he and Shirley enjoyed a poignant reunion together with each of their families. They didn't know when they would get a chance to see the children again and they hungrily savored every available minute.

Twelve family members, as well as friends from South Africa, gathered to bid them farewell. Talking for hours and hours, the group reflected on the memories they shared. There were many wet tissues and just as much laughter. Hugs and hand-holding. Expressions of fear and bursts of uncontainable excitement.

Among the other relatives in attendance, Shirley was forced to say good-bye to her only granddaughter, Adie. Only six months old, she couldn't understand what was going on around her. Tears slid down Shirley's sad, smiling face as she looked at the tiny, beautiful baby and wondered when she would ever see her again.

Far too soon, on the evening of December 27, 1986, it was time to embark upon their flight to Tel Aviv. They decided to take advantage of an early check-in service offered by the airlines at a major hotel outside of Johannesburg. Borrowing one car, and with Marlene following in her vehicle filled with the rest of their belongings, Gary and Shirley made their way to the check-in location.

A long line was already forming when they arrived. It moved painfully slowly. Shirley held their place in the queue as Gary began the arduous task of organizing their eighteen heavy, space-consuming pieces of luggage. Sliding step by step, they patiently waited while other people pushed their luggage along, each time the line inched forward. An hour later, it was finally their turn to be checked in.

"I'm sorry," the attendant told them firmly, raising an eyebrow at the mountain of belongings in front of her, "you cannot check in eighteen pieces of luggage. Airline policy restricts passengers to two pieces each plus carry-on items."

"But we're making *aliyah*," Gary beseeched her. "We need all of this to make a new home."

The attendant looked carefully at Gary and Shirley, again surveying the massive bulk of suitcases and parcels. Shaking her head, she excused herself, asking them, please, to wait a moment. She would go speak to the manager and get his opinion.

While she was gone, Gary and Shirley talked animatedly between themselves. Suddenly, a porter arrived and began, automatically, to load their luggage. In the process of waiting, some of it had already been ticketed for arrival in Israel and the suitcases appeared to be ready for transport.

Gary tapped the man on the shoulder. "Excuse me, but we're waiting for authorization to take all this with us on our trip."

"Certainly. That's fine, sir. While you're waiting, I'll get most of it loaded up. Make things easier for you."

Gary looked at Shirley; she smiled back. Both were a bit confused, but this seemed to be a delightful sign from the Lord that they would be allowed to overstep the baggage limits.

The porter took the ticketed baggage and placed it in a freight van to be taken to the airport. Then, with a wave, he was quickly out of sight.

By the time the ticketing agent returned with the manager in tow, half the luggage was nowhere to be seen, on its way to the airplane. What remained was counted, and the manager found only nine pieces total despite the conversation he'd already had with the attendant. Frowning, he asked, "I thought there was more than this. Why do you need to bring so much to Israel?"

Patiently, Gary repeated that they were immigrating. They needed all of these belongings to settle into their new home. The other pieces, he explained, had already been taken away.

The manager waved his hands in the air and smiled expansively, as if Gary's explanation made the defining difference. "Well, then," he beamed, "that's wonderful! God bless you and I hope you enjoy your flight."

The ticket agent was advised to okay the Beresfords' luggage for transport, and Gary and Shirley were cleared for departure. Once again, they realized, God had paved the way for their trip to Israel. Only through his guidance could such a confused situation be remedied so easily.

They had some time left before they had to board their plane, so they returned to Marlene's house. Unencumbered by their luggage, they were finally able to enjoy a few unexpected hours of camaraderie with family and friends. When the clock finally indicated that they needed to go to the airport, they tearfully said their final good-byes.

These good-byes, indeed, could be final.

Chapter Ten

IN THE LAND

The plane prepared to touch down upon Israeli soil. Outside their window, Gary and Shirley caught sight of patches of gray-blue sky through a mass of dense clouds. As they approached the landing strip, the scene that greeted them was carved of old stone, everywhere, with occasional splotches of bright and welcoming greenery. Modern structures were interspersed with ancient history.

Excitedly, Gary and Shirley spoke about the man who would meet them at the airport. They had met him in Zimbabwe at a Christian Friends of Israel function at which they had been guest speakers. Visiting from the Ivory Coast, he had announced that he would be in Israel on business at the end of December.

"It would be my honor," he had energetically assured the

Beresfords, "to meet you at the airport upon your arrival in Israel." He would take care of everything, even going so far as to arrange for their transportation and accommodations. Anything and everything they might need upon arrival would be handled; there was no reason to be concerned about the start of their stay in the land.

On the ground and finally out of the plane, Gary and Shirley were swept along amidst a mass of impatient passengers also being processed into the country. Jostling each other, the bulk of bodies shuffled together towards a common, eagerly anticipated goal. All needed to pass through Customs control to be granted legal entry into the country.

Gary and Shirley were issued the standard three-month visitor's visas, and then they moved into the Customs area. Recalling the lively baggage check-in they'd experienced in Johannesburg, both were convinced that Israeli Customs would be as inquisitive as the South African airline personnel had been. After all, it was unlikely that a couple would bring so large an amount of personal possessions into the country for nothing more than a vacation.

To their amazement, officials made few remarks over their mound of luggage, asking Gary only about a hand-held steel filing case he carried. He said that inside the file were personal papers. The official asked Gary to open it and after the contents were thoroughly checked, the customs official smiled, nodded, and waved them on. In their minds, this was yet another sign from God that he wanted them in Israel. No trouble at the gates.

It was time to go looking for their friend in the airport arrival area. Standing there, luggage surrounding them like a small fortress, they searched the sea of faces swimming past for sight of their contact.

He was nowhere to be found.

He must simply be late, they decided, and awkwardly settled into nearby seats and continued to observe and wait for his familiar face to materialize. One hour turned into two and still the man had not arrived. Two hours dreadfully stretched into even more and they finally allowed themselves to admit their concern; worry mirrored in each other's expressions. This was most definitely not going as planned.

"Let's face it. He's not coming!" Shirley's voice burst forth with the frustration they both felt. Tears welled in her eyes and ran down her face. Looking skyward, she beseeched, "What now, Lord? What will we do?" Then to Gary, "What *will* we do? Why didn't we make our own preparations?"

Gary was at a loss for words. He, too, felt the despondency, the overwhelming loneliness of being in a new country with not even a single comforting face to greet them. Neither knew very much Hebrew, nor were they familiar with the specific customs of the Israeli people. It was mid-winter, cold, and they sat in a foreign airport with very little money, few communication skills, and nowhere to go.

No longer did they have a home in Zimbabwe. Now, they found themselves set adrift in a land about which they knew virtually nothing. Suddenly they wondered how they could have been so naive as to trust a virtual stranger to take care of their arrival needs.

Yet they had. They were here. And something had to be done. Gary was determined not to give in to his doubts. Padding his voice with unfelt determination so as not to give his wife more fuel for her fears, he did his best to comfort her. Refusing to allow his voice to waver, he managed a small smile and responded, "We'll manage, love." He took hold of Shirley's hand. "We will manage...with God's help," he repeated, half to himself, half to God.

Nodding, Shirley took a firm grasp of Gary's hand. Homeless, scared, exhausted, cold, hungry, yet amidst her physical frustrations, she was given an immediate answer to her earlier question—"What will we do?"

The Lord's voice came to her, as it had another time in immediate response to her concerns about physical comfort. The voice was firm, strong, solid, as he instructed, "*Never* look at the circumstances; always keep your eyes on me."

A sigh came out from deep within her and Gary looked over, concern creasing his brow. "No," she assured him, "don't worry about me. Don't worry about what we will do next. It will be okay." She patted his hand again. "The Lord wants us here. It will be okay." With her free hand, Shirley wiped the moisture from her face.

We must look a sight, they reflected, sitting huddled together holding on to each other, their mountain of baggage all around them, Shirley's tear-stained face now alight with a tentative, relieved smile. They remained that way awhile, praying quietly that the Lord would show them what to do for accommodations for the evening. The future would be contended with after a good night's rest.

"I think I know what we can do." The solution hadn't taken long to come to him. Gary gently removed his hand from Shirley's to reach for his billfold. Pulling out a small slip of paper, he declared with certainty, "Here is our answer, love."

While in prayer, he had remembered that they had been given the name, address, and phone number of a young man who managed the Beit Emmanuel hostel in Jaffa. The man's cousin had offered them the information a week before they left for Israel, assuring them that if they needed anything, they could call his cousin, Akiva, a Jewish believer.

They proceeded to try and do so, discovering in the process that placing a telephone call in Israel required special tokens called *asimonim.* With the language barrier working severely against them, they had a hard time finding out where to purchase the tokens. Eventually the couple found a place and spent a half an hour dialing Akiva's phone number. The line was continuously busy.

Shirley was shivering and having a hard time keeping her eyes open. Then and there, Gary decided not to wait any longer for the phone line to clear. They were both fatigued and overwhelmed from their flight and the mounting tensions of their present circumstances.

They would approach Akiva in person. They had already spent too much time worrying and waiting. Worrying was useless, waiting wasted good time.

Gary went out in front of the airport, where the taxis and busses lined up, and quickly hired a large commuter taxi—a *sherut*—whose driver was willing to take them and their belongings to the hostel.

During the twenty minute ride, they became a part of the heavy traffic of Sunday, Israel's first workday of the week. Cars and busses filled the roads, honking horns, passing under traffic lights, barely waiting as pedestrians dangerously wended their ways between moving and parked vehicles.

Their taxi eventually turned off the highway and entered bustling, downtown Jaffa. Crammed with ancient buildings and tiny, unkempt, cluttered storefronts, the streets were barely wide enough for even the smallest vehicle. The driver twisted and turned in countless directions, people scurrying about alone or in small groups, intent on their daily business. The overall atmosphere was that of the Old World one reads about in history books—foreign, frightening, yet very exciting.

Arriving, finally, at their destination, the taxi pulled into the hostel's parking lot. The large rectangular building, made of smooth, finished stone, was set in a residential area facing a Lutheran church. The "history book" feel also carried over to this area. A fine rain was beginning to wash down on them as Gary and Shirley exited the taxi, their belongings carried along slowly by them and their driver.

Inside, after the driver had been paid and sent on his way, they asked to see Akiva. While they waited, they walked around and curiously looked at the room's sparse furnishings, old but clean. Moments later, Akiva approached and introduced himself.

"We are the Beresfords," Gary began. "We met your cousin, Jeff, in Johannesburg last week. He encouraged us to contact you for a place to stay upon our arrival in Israel. We were supposed to have been met by someone who would have made these arrangements for us, but he never arrived."

Akiva expressed his sympathy and the three of them began to discuss the matter in detail. Akiva was understanding and kind. However, the hostel was fully booked; there was not one room available. He didn't see how he could help.

Literally, there was no room at the inn.

Gary took a deep, steadying breath. Both he and Shirley were wet; she was still shivering. She looked as if she was about to break down and cry. "Please," Gary begged, "we've just flown all the way from South Africa." Gary tried to remain calm. "We are chilled from being outside, we have eighteen pieces of luggage, and we are extremely tired and worn out. Is there nothing you can do for us?"

Lifting his hands palm up in supplication, Akiva thought again. "I'll tell you what I *can* do," he responded after a few moments of silence. "If you're willing to sleep in my apartment with me, I can put Shirley in the ladies' dormitory. There is one bed unoccupied to which she is certainly welcome. This is the most I can do until a single room becomes available, probably in a day or two."

It was not the way Gary and Shirley had envisioned their first night in Israel. At this point, however, they were entirely thankful for a roof over their heads, a bed where they could rest their battered bodies, and a safe place to store their luggage. Gratefully, they accepted Akiva's offer.

□□□

Days later, still at the Beit Emmanuel hostel, but now in a private room together, Gary and Shirley took a bus to Jerusalem. They were going to apply for citizenship at the Ministry of Interior. They had re-contacted Gary's cousin, John, and he had agreed to let them use his address for all correspondence since they were uncertain from one day to the next where they would be staying.

Completing the paperwork, they were informed that the

process usually took one month, after which they would be asked to return to the offices for a consultation on the reasons behind their desire to immigrate. Once this procedure was fulfilled, they would be notified in writing regarding the status of their immigrant visas. The two had already faced so many roadblocks just to get into Israel, they prayed their troubles were finally behind them.

In a month, they were certain, they would learn of their impending Israeli citizenship. Finally, Gary and Shirley Beresford would have a country, a home, a place where they felt they truly belonged. Then they could begin their new life, free to fully immerse themselves in Israeli society. They had been divinely called to this country.

This was what God wanted of them, right?

□□□

As they awaited word on their application, Gary and Shirley began to make friends, among them Akiva and his girlfriend. On Akiva's recommendation, the Beresfords attended a lecture given by Dr. Michael Brown, a guest speaker from the United States, at the Ramat HaSharon Messianic Congregation just north of Tel Aviv. Akiva and his girlfriend would meet them there.

The evening of the lecture, they boarded a bus from Jaffa to the Central Bus Station in Tel Aviv, then transferred to the Ramat HaSharon bus. The bus let them off just outside of town, between two strawberry fields. It was darkening and, after searching on foot for nearly an hour, they located the obscure road—Dust Road—which led to the meeting.

The door was opened by a young Israeli lady. After introducing themselves, Gary and Shirley were ushered into a large room packed with other men and women. In muted whispers, they were offered two empty chairs. The speaker had already begun.

His subject was the importance of maintaining a strong Jewish identity. He stressed that, in present society, the Torah had not been done away with but, in truth, was being upheld by the strength of conviction of a constantly growing number of Jewish believers throughout the world. An in-depth explanation was given on the New Testament as it related to the Old Testament in light of God's commandments.

As Gary and Shirley listened, their rapt attention focused on the speaker and his engaging words. Gary realized the enormous significance of what it meant to be part of a Messianic Jewish congregation. This kind of interaction would be crucial to the continuance of their new faith-filled lifestyle.

He understood, with more clarity than ever before, that their Jewish identity certainly did *not* need to be renounced since they had declared faith in Yeshua as Messiah. It was evident, even only after a short amount of time with these people, that here was a group where they might find the nurturing and learning experiences they needed and desired.

With the speech concluded, there was a time of socializing, giving them a chance to get to know some of the people around them. Gary and Shirley were introduced to Ari and Shira Sorko-Ram, the couple in whose home the congregation met. Their personal style was warm; Ari and Shira invited the Beresfords to become part of the congregation, which met every Tuesday evening.

Gary began to explain to the Sorko-Rams how he and Shirley had recently arrived in Israel from South Africa and had applied for Israeli citizenship. "Presently we're staying at the Beit Emmanuel hostel, but soon we'll need to find more permanent living accommodations. Unfortunately," he grimaced, "our finances are extremely limited while we're in this state of uncertainty."

"Come," Ari gestured, smiling as he led them toward an older gentleman standing nearby, "let me introduce you to someone. Gary and Shirley Beresford, this is Paul." Ari apprised the man of the Beresfords' situation, adding that he thought Paul might be able to be of some help.

"Indeed." Paul warmly shook hands with Gary and Shirley.

His smile was genuine and inviting. "I have a very large house in Hod HaSharon. You're welcome to stay with me. I have more than enough room, and would enjoy the company while my wife is away visiting family in Canada. Remain as long as it takes for you to find your own home." Shirley couldn't believe her ears. She returned Paul's smile and hugged him, expressing her enthusiastic thanks. Gary was relieved to know that they would be able to move out of the hostel and into an environment with more privacy. This would make their search for a house of their own a more comfortable and pleasant endeavor.

Two days later, Paul arrived at Beit Emmanuel hostel with a friend, Baruch, in tow. The Beresfords' luggage was loaded into his vehicle, Gary and Shirley climbed in behind it, and the four of them drove off.

□□□

Life with Paul was pleasant and peaceful. Paul was retired, allowing him a good amount of freedom to spend with his new house guests. He had no children living in Israel and his wife was away on an extended visit. Gary and Shirley felt that he seemed lonely in his big house by himself; their presence provided him the company he needed.

Paul was more than willing to show them how to assimilate into Israeli life and explained everything in great detail. His help was invaluable as he took them around to the local supermarkets and open air markets, explaining local customs and laws. Paul introduced the couple to his friends who, in turn, became their friends, also. He even showed Gary and Shirley how to begin an elementary Hebrew home study course.

By the end of their fourth week with Paul, they still patiently awaited a response from the Ministry of the Interior concerning the status of their immigration request. Not a single word had been heard. Not a piece of mail had been received.

Soon it was almost six weeks since they'd moved into Paul's house, and longer since they'd applied for immigration, Gary and Shirley's patience began to wear thin. They made phone calls to the Ministry office and were repeatedly put off with empty words and promises for follow-up. It became more and more evident by the silent passing of time on the part of the Israeli government, that the Beresfords' request was not going through with ease.

Gary and Shirley approached their new friends, the Sorko-Rams, and asked for advice. Once again they explained how and why the Zionist Federation in South Africa had earlier turned down their initial request for immigration.

"I'd be very concerned, too," Ari agreed, after hearing the story. "It would appear that the Ministry has heard of your belief in Yeshua."

"Do you really think this will make a difference? It shouldn't."

"No, it shouldn't, but it already has. Look at the facts. Look at how long it's taken. You have heard nothing. They won't accept your phone calls. Yes," he nodded resolutely, "I'd say they're avoiding you. The Zionist Federation must have contacted them."

"What would *you* do?"

Ari looked at Shira, then spoke. "I know a lawyer who might help. If you pursue this legally, then anything they do, they must answer for."

Gary put his arm around Shirley. She leaned her head against his shoulder. "I suppose you're right. We're not going to go away, and they have to realize that."

□□□

Gary and Shirley made an appointment with Joseph Ben-Menashe, the lawyer to whom Ari had referred them. Mr. Ben-Menashe was willing to see them quickly. Awaiting their consultation, sitting outside near the reception area, they could feel the nervous energy flow between them.

The attorney arrived and invited them inside his office. After exchanging pleasantries, Gary and Shirley explained the sequence of events which had brought them to him. They told of how they had been repeatedly ignored by the Ministry of the Interior. The government, in their opinion, was offering them no alternative but to proceed legally. The situation must be pursued until it was satisfactorily resolved. They intended to immigrate to Israel under the Law of Return and the Israeli government would have to recognize them.

Mr. Ben-Menashe agreed that the officials seemed to be stalling. He said he would send a letter to the Ministry of the Interior requesting a definitive reply to the Beresfords' application for citizenship within two weeks. He promised that he would keep them informed concerning each move by him and the government. They would soon have their answer.

□ □ □

Time passed. No news was *not* good news.

"We *still* haven't heard, have we?" Gary asked his attorney over the phone. "The two weeks are up, and no answer. What can be done?"

Chapter Eleven

TAKE IT TO COURT

Time continued without word from the Ministry of the Interior. In March 1987, the Beresfords' attorney prepared to appear before Israel's High Court of Justice for an order that would compel the Ministry of the Interior to answer his letter within forty-five days either favorably, by granting the couple citizenship, or to show cause for their denial.

No longer was there any doubt as to what was going on. The Beresfords were being ignored. Now it was time to make the government explain why.

A friend drove them to the Supreme Court building, a decrepit structure situated in the Russian Compound in Jerusalem, not far from the Old City. The building's facade cried out for refurbishing, and probably had for decades. A stern, imposing Russian Orthodox church stood diagonally across the street, its menacing domes towering over the area with a suggestion of authority. The overall landscape appeared oppressive, dark, hopeless.

Gary and Shirley entered the building hand-in-hand, fingers entwined in nervousness. The military security within didn't help lighten their moods. Shirley was asked to open her purse and all its contents were carefully surveyed. Gary was grilled to see whether or not he carried a weapon. Both knew that this was normal procedure in a country that often suffered terrorist attacks.

Finally able to clear the security area, they found Mr. Ben-Menashe standing directly outside the courtroom reading through documents. Within moments, they were invited inside the courtroom. They took seats located in the back. Theirs was not the only case to be heard that day, and other petitioners filed in around them. Personal conversations went on behind and in front of them, everyone concerned with his own individual needs.

The benches were hard, wooden, backless, not made for comfort. The tiny room was spartan; inside it, everyone looked like a poor plaintiff. Gary and Shirley sat, still holding hands, when a side door opened inward. A clerk demanded all rise as three judges entered solemnly to make their way to the judge's bench, which sat as the center of attention at the front of the room.

The Beresfords' uneasiness was not allayed. Two cases preceded theirs. Finding it impossible to follow due to the language barrier, it was only through the translations of their friend that they learned what was going on.

The judges began to hear the case just before theirs. A young man stood before the court. He had no desire to fight in the Israeli Army, he declared; thus, he wished to give up his identity as an Israeli and a Jew. He was more than willing to have his citizenship revoked, so that he could legally refuse to serve in the country's armed forces. If relinquishing his citizenship was necessary to keep him out of the Israeli Army, he was quite agreeable.

The irony that this case preceded theirs did not escape Gary or Shirley. If it had not been so hard for their emotions to grasp that someone was *trying* to not be a Jewish citizen in Israel—on purpose—the Beresfords might actually have found the entire scenario laughable.

Yet here they were, wanting nothing more than to be considered Jews in the eyes of the Israeli courts. They were willing to do everything asked of them by the Israeli government in order to achieve this goal. In contrast, a young man was in front of them apparently throwing away that very same privilege. He obviously didn't comprehend that what he was so willing to relinquish was, in fact, a precious honor.

Forty-five minutes of confrontation, arguing, and obvious disappointment ensued. Finally, the young man left the courtroom and it was time for the Beresfords' case to be heard.

Mr. Ben-Menashe rose to his feet to respectfully address the judges. His words gained momentum as he gave firm voice to the Beresfords' request for citizenship and the surrounding circumstances which precipitated this request; then he asked that the issue be swiftly and finally addressed.

No chance. There was a brief deliberation between both sides. Then the judges gave the Ministry, whose representatives listened quietly and politely, forty-five days in which to respond to the Beresfords' petition.

Another delay. Forty-five more days! Gary had a hard time controlling his frustration and emotions. He felt his face grow hot as he struggled to retain his civility and manners. He looked, pleading, at the judges; they returned his stare, unmoved. Then he turned to face Shirley; pain and outrage evident in her eyes. Surely this was beyond any common sense understanding. What had they done to deserve such treatment?

□□□

A restless conversation took place late that night as Gary and Shirley lay in bed, focusing on their present hardships. Again and again they marveled at how the knowledge of their belief in Yeshua had found its way to so many people, so quickly. Even stranger was how defending this one point had become so pivotal in the legal maneuvers they had been forced to undertake. It had become the focus of everything they said and did.

The couple relived the various events which had led up to this point, attempting to piece together from where the news had originated.

"The Hebrew Order of David," Gary suggested, as the thought came to him. "Our former 'friends.' They ate with us, had Shabbat with us, played tennis with us; yet we already know that behind our backs they advised the Federation of our newfound beliefs. Who knows? Maybe they took it even farther, beyond the Federation."

"There was also that man who stayed in our home for a few weeks," Shirley suggested, indicating a young, traitorous guest whom they had at one time housed. "He, too, entered our home as a friend yet left loudly and rudely claiming a disgust in what we stood for."

They finally realized in their hearts that it no longer mattered how news had gotten around; now there were political machinations behind the delays. Nothing within their own power could move things forward. It was out of their hands. They prayed for much-needed patience and guidance, finally allowing sleep to settle in. They had to rest, to try to relax, until the forty-five days of the court delay were over.

□□□

The language barrier had been a difficult one for both of them since they had first stepped onto Israeli soil with the intention of staying. As a visitor, it was an irritation to not be able to capably speak the language; as someone living in the country, it was next to impossible to function without at least understanding the basics. They had both taken the brief, elementary Hebrew course suggested by Paul, but it had covered only a little of what was required for daily life.

To combat this problem, Gary enrolled in an *ulpan*, a Hebrew language school. In Ra'ananna, a neighboring town, he attended classes six days a week for five months, eventually learning enough conversational Hebrew to get by. This single triumph made their lives easier and more comfortable emotionally. It afforded opportunities for important friendships with both immigrants and native Israelis.

Twice in that period their lawyer had received requests from the Ministry for time extensions, and he advised the Beresfords to agree to them. He was thinking of the future. In the event they eventually needed to take this to trial, their attorney believed that the Ministry would be hard pressed not to reciprocate the courtesy if extensions were required on their side. Gary and Shirley followed his advice. Sixty days after they began the proceedings, they would receive their initial answer.

It was beginning to seem as if they might make an occupation out of their determination to live in Israel. If this was how it was going to be—a distinct possibility as things stood—the Beresfords felt as if they needed permanent accommodations within the land, as permanent as their situation presently allowed.

Living with Paul was a gift. He was a wonderful friend and an accommodating landlord but, no matter how much he tried to make it easy for them, it was still someone else's home. They needed a retreat of their own, at least some semblance of it for personal stability.

Together on Paul's balcony, wistfully overlooking the uneven rooftops and handmade gardens of the surrounding homes, their sights came to rest on a house across the street. It had stood vacant the entire time they had been with Paul and they had often admired it curiously from a distance. He had advised them that it belonged to the woman who developed the neighborhood.

"Paul," Shirley called, walking back inside with a single objective.

"Yes?" He was in the kitchen.

Shirley stood straight in the doorway. Her voice was strong as she spoke. "That house across the street. It would be so nice for Gary and me to live in. It's close to you, and we do love this area. How do we inquire about renting it?"

Paul firmly shook his head, trying to ward off her hopeful determination. He could see from the thoughtful frown creasing her forehead that she would not be easily dissuaded. "Shirley," his eyes narrowed, "you'll need a miracle to live there. The owner will never rent. Never. She wants to keep it available for herself."

"So you don't think there's any chance?"

"Not that I can see. In the three years since it was built, no one has lived there. Not even she. I really doubt she'll ever change her mind on how she wants to handle the occupancy of that house, whether she ever resides in it or not."

Shirley, however, was not to be deterred. Gary, knowing his wife's sense of purpose, agreed to have a go at discussing the matter with the real estate agent who represented the home's owner. Its exterior was well-kept and attractive, the size was just perfect for them, and they had become most comfortable living in that area.

Gary contacted the real estate agent. True to Paul's words, Gary was told unquestionably that the owner was not the least bit willing to discuss a rental. He had, of course, expected this answer; yet he persisted in his inquiry, refusing to take a "no" from the agent alone. Reluctantly, seemingly to get Gary off the phone, the agent finally agreed to check with his client to see if she would change her mind.

Two days later he called for the Beresfords at Paul's house. His voice betrayed amazement as he related that his client had agreed to rent her home to this determined couple. If they would come into his office and fill out the rental agreement, they could move in on a two-year lease as soon as they were ready.

At this point, the Beresfords' belongings were in storage at the port of Ashdod on the Mediterranean coast. Gary arranged to have the shipment cleared, but shipping agents subsequently denied his request because he and Shirley possessed only tourist status in Israel. Tourists, they explained, were not allowed to move into the country. Bringing personal property into Israel implied intended residency, and the law required that one must already be a citizen, a permanent resident, or possess a work permit to import large amounts of personal property.

What would they do now? They had signed a contract to rent a home, but had nothing with which to furnish it. They hadn't made allowances for this problem; the possibility that they wouldn't be allowed to retrieve their own belongings had never entered their mind. In addition, if they couldn't get their things out of storage, they would be required to continue paying one thousand *shekels* a month in storage fees—approximately five hundred U.S. dollars. Expenses were mounting, they had neither employment nor permits to work, and their battle for citizenship had hardly begun.

It seemed as if they would have to become accustomed to—if not comfortable with—a lifestyle of hardship and uncertainty.

□□□

Gary and Shirley had to acknowledge that some of their uncertainness stemmed from the suddenness of their decision to move. Yet just as much of it was due to obstacles placed in their way by others—both knowingly and unknowingly. It seemed as if every corner turned revealed another stumbling block. Life had become a study in problem-solving.

And so, without furniture or personal belongings, the two braved the circumstances and moved into the house across the street from Paul in March of 1987. Friends and neighbors, sympathetic to their plight, offered help in every way possible, lending odds and ends to provide life's bare necessities. It might not be homey, but it would still be their home.

Then, all at once, they knew. Finally, the answer had come to the question that had been haunting them. The answer was "no." The Ministry of the Interior had turned down their request and, in the process, made a bed of sorrow for Gary and Shirley. They looked at the contents of the letter in disbelief. Shirley's son, Javin, had given them over to the Ministry officials. Javin had betrayed them, and now they were suffering the consequences by being barred from becoming Israeli citizens.

They were forced to make their next move with care. The evidence of Javin's betrayal was impossible to ignore. It was a hurt they were forced to carry, one from which they could not hide. His actions would define their future countermoves; they had to face reality soberly, for it was a reality that they were no longer able to escape.

Over the next month they discussed their situation with Ari and Shira and other friends, constantly praying to find out what the Lord's desire was for them.

Shirley managed to hold her own, exhibiting to the world a steely resolve. Precariously, she balanced her personal pain with the comfort and strength of Gary's unwavering presence beside her. That, along with the certainty that the Lord was with them both, assured her that they would make it through.

The Beresfords were reminded by their attorney that their current tourist visas were soon to expire. If they planned to continue their fight, they had to renew those visas immediately. They had already done so once before. Given the recent decision against them, it was unlikely that another extension would be granted. They felt like enemies of the State, harassed for undefined crimes.

It was during a conversation with Ari and Shira that Gary and Shirley began to get a feel for how the Ministry's negative decision—and even Javin's betrayal—might somehow be turned around and used by the Lord in bringing his people back to Israel.

One night at the Sorko-Rams' home, feeling vulnerable, hurt, and unsure, they talked of how all the deceit and hardheartedness against them had deeply affected them, emotionally and physically. They felt tired, sapped of the strength they needed. They didn't know how much more they could take. They were, after all, only human.

"We don't have the financial resources to engage in a lengthy lawsuit," Gary stressed, his hands spread wide over the table in front of him. "Neither do we have theological expertise, nor the knowledge to adequately present our case against the Ministry's declaration that we've converted to another religion. We *know* we've not done so, but how do we present that in a legal format? Really, it's a theological issue!"

"Yes, you *are* still Jews" Shira assured them, "and, as Jews, you have every right to make *aliyah*. You know we'll be here for you no matter what you need. As leaders of the congregation, we'll help with every spiritual and material resource we have available to us."

"Have you considered," Ari added thoughtfully, "that this struggle may be used by God? He might utilize it to dismantle the prevailing attitude in the Israeli government toward the Messianic Jews. It could become a source of strength and inspiration to future Jewish believers who wish to immigrate to their homeland. People just like you."

A dawning ray of hope gave meaning and reason to the seeming insanity of their situation. It had not occurred to Gary nor to Shirley that their plight could be used in such a sweeping, important fashion.

They had always believed that the Lord had directed them to Israel and that he continued to encourage them in their fight to stay despite the mounting opposition. They had never considered that they could be a part of God's greater plan in such an overwhelming way.

"Are you willing and strong enough to be the Lord's vessel?" Ari asked. He searched both Gary and Shirley's faces, looking for confirmation. His own expression remained stern, impassive, projecting the importance of what he was saying. "You have to know what you're getting into. Are you each willing to go wherever the

Lord leads, do whatever he requires no matter what happens. If you are, be sure to approach this with your eyes completely open."

The enormity of their task lay before them. It was monumental. To answer "yes" would be to pit themselves against a strongly held, generally accepted tenet of Judaism. Perhaps it was simply too much to ask. Gary and Shirley remained still, silently considering Ari's words. Their response, no matter which it was, would lead them on to the next stage in their lives.

But it was this monumental idea, this enormous task, this undeniable reality into which they had been thrust, which said "continue." It was not really an option. It was a command. It was a sense that they were part of a movement and a cause larger than their own struggle. And in this realization Gary and Shirley discovered a purpose they had never known before.

□□□

True to his avowal to help, Ari immediately made arrangements to speak directly with the Beresfords' lawyer. He wanted to personally understand the full scope of what they were up against. Next, he contacted Dr. David Stern, a well-respected Messianic Jewish theologian, and Joseph Shulam, a Messianic congregational leader and theologian, both of whom were Israeli citizens, residing in Jerusalem.

He asked if they would be willing to meet and discuss the Beresfords' plight, with an eye towards planning a strategy to keep them in the country and ultimately secure their citizenship. Each was agreeable, and Gary and Shirley found peace and excitement in this. Strangers were going out of their way to help with a cause, their cause, one in which they all believed. For the weary warriors, it came as a motivating and invigorating revitalization.

One point was becoming obvious. The pervading and growing negative atmosphere towards Messianic Jews was making it increasingly difficult and potentially dangerous to stand up for their cause. Visible or vocal support could be a risk to any well-respected individual, within or without of the Messianic world. Rocking the proverbial boat was not going to be a popular practice.

The group assembled by Ari was organized to design a plan for the Beresfords to make their case more widely known and supported. It was decided that Gary and Shirley should fight the Ministry of the Interior by asking the High Court of Justice to compel the Ministry of the Interior to grant them *oleh* (Jewish immigrant) status under the Law of Return. Their attorney was consulted about a strategy, and Gary and Shirley petitioned for a hearing. A date was set allowing for both sides to accumulate evidence. After a series of granted extensions, a final trial date was set.

The Beresfords continued in their determination that they would ultimately win the right to reside in Israel. The battle had taken on greater dimensions than they had ever thought possible, yet they were in it for the duration. They would never give up. If the Lord willed it—and they were certain now that he wanted this as much as they did—they *would* live in the Promised Land as the Jews they knew themselves to be.

Chapter Twelve

HOPE ALMOST LOST

Their court case against the Ministry of the Interior was not the only concern in their lives. They had made many friends and found life in general as Messianic Jews in Israel to be both fulfilling and time-consuming.

Dr. David Stern was carefully following the proceedings and considering what else he could do to help. In the past, there had been at least three other similar cases [see Appendix] which had been tried in the High Court of Justice—one in 1962, another in 1970, and a third in 1978. Dr. Stern was intrigued by how the Court seemed to take a theory that had arisen from the 1962 court case and hold it up as a precedent in the Beresford case.

In 1962, the High Court of Justice had ruled against Oswald Rufeysen, known as Brother Daniel, a Jewish Carmelite monk who called himself "a Jew by nationality and a Roman Catholic by religion." He too had wanted to make *aliyah* under the Law of Return, but was rejected by the court on the ground that even though he had a Jewish mother and, thus, was Jewish according to *halakhah*, the secular State of Israel was not bound by Jewish religious law. Therefore, the state could use other criteria to determine who should be considered a Jew for purposes of the Law of Return.

The criterion used for the Brother Daniel case was based on the "man-on-the-street" theory. It indicated that if Brother Daniel, wearing a brown monk's robe and a cross around his neck, were seen in the streets of Tel Aviv, he would not be viewed as a Jew. Based upon that, the court ruled, he was not one.

The Ministry of the Interior was now updating the theory to apply to the Beresfords' case. They claimed that the average man-on-the-street would likewise not view the Beresfords as Jews because they followed a religious leader who was *seen as* "the Christian Messiah." Thus, said the court, the Beresfords were no longer Jewish.

It occurred to Dr. Stern, however, that so long as no one had inquired of the *real* Jew-on-the-street, he might be depicted as having any opinion convenient to make a desired argument. Who could challenge that which had no tangible basis? Yet, if a research institute highly reputable in scientific competence and lacking religious bias were to conduct a proper survey of public opinion there would no longer be any room for uncertainty.

Thus, in January of 1988, the Dahaf Research Institute of Tel Aviv was asked to conduct such a survey. Interviews were conducted face-to-face with 1,189 Jewish Israelis. They were presented with a statement which summarized the Law of Return, explaining that this definition could be open to various interpretations.

Ten categories of possible immigrants were listed and interviewees were asked the following question about each of the categories: "In your opinion, does the person described...have the right to receive an immigrant's visa under the Law of Return?"

The survey's response was overwhelming. An absolute majority of the public expressing opinions (more than fifty percent) favored granting an immigrant's visa under the Law of Return to all categories, even someone "born to a Jewish mother and baptized in the framework of a Christian church." A full eighty-two percent of those with opinions supported the Messianic Jew who affirmed his loyalty to his people and to the State of Israel. Overall, it was determined that the public wanted only the reassurance that the immigrant could prove he was a Jew and had never been a traitor to his people. Their concern was not with how that immigrant did or did not practice his Jewishness.

The "man-on-the-street" theory had been publicly put to the test and the High Court's assumptions were found wanting. The results were rushed to the attorney to be included in the Beresfords' file only a few days before they were to go to court and present their case. Potent material. Or so they thought.

The judges saw the poll for the first time during the February 1988 trial, and from their facial expressions as they read, it was clear that the results surprised them. But would this change the outcome? The trial went on for several hours and was finally "continued" to a date in May.

Meanwhile, in the spring of 1988, Gary and Shirley were asked by Ari and Shira to serve as the Israeli coordinators for an international conference to be held in Jerusalem during Shavuot, the Feast of Weeks.

The Messianic Jewish Alliance of America and the Union of Messianic Jewish Congregations, two organizations headquartered in the United States, were sponsoring this international conference in conjunction with a host of Israeli believers. Gary and Shirley were eager to take on the positions offered to them. First, though, they had to apply for, and be granted, Israeli work permits.

"It's so ironic," Gary laughed one evening as he and Shirley left a conference planning meeting, to their surprise, having been granted a work permit. "We've been denied so much in this country because of our faith in Yeshua. Yet, we've been granted the chance to be involved with an international Messianic Jewish conference whose central purpose is to proclaim in this country Yeshua as the Jewish Messiah!"

Daily, as conference efforts unfolded, Gary and Shirley had their first real glimpse of how massive and encompassing the international Messianic Jewish movement was. They had the privilege of meeting believers from all backgrounds and facets of Messianic life. People came from every corner of Israel, as well as from South America, Australia, New Zealand, North America, Africa, and Europe.

It was the Beresfords' job to ensure that each one of these people had accommodations. They booked the entire Diplomat Hotel in Jerusalem, complete with a conference hall that seated twelve hundred. When the reservation list was checked prior to the conference, it was discovered that there were too many applicants for the Diplomat to house. Rooms were quickly booked at two other hotels, with adjoining meeting space and closed-circuit television for overflow crowds. The total attendance of 1,400, half of whom were Messianic Jews and the other half "Messianic gentiles"—that is, gentile Christians—made this probably the largest gathering of Jewish believers in Yeshua since the first centuries of the Common Era.

The first evening of the conference arrived just after the second High Court trial date, at which time the rest of the evidence was heard. All that remained was for the judges to give their verdict. At the conference, Gary and Shirley were able to temporarily put aside their legal problems, becoming enthralled by the marvelous insights of the various speakers. Attendees leaned forward in their seats, soaking in every word, taking notes. The worship experience was beyond all expectations, complete with international and Israeli musical artists.

The excited, inspired couple were prepared to be as equally

stimulated the next evening. They listened to more speakers and participated in expressive worship times of prayer, song, and dance. As the music died down, everyone found a seat and Sid Roth, Master of Ceremonies and founder of Messianic Vision, a well-respected Messianic Jewish organization from the United States, approached the podium.

"This year we have with us a couple whose beliefs in Yeshua have brought them from South Africa to Israel," Sid began.

Gary looked at Shirley. She shook her head as if to say she was as surprised as he. They fine-tuned their attention, awaiting Sid's next words.

"Mr. and Mrs. Gary Beresford want to live out the rest of their lives in the land. They wish to become Israeli citizens, to offer their skills and abilities to build up this country promised to the Jews, God's chosen people. Yet they are finding that their road to immigration is paved with ever-increasing financial hardships and legal difficulties due, mostly, to the legal roadblocks put in their way by the Israeli government."

Sid briefly explained what was happening with the storage of the Beresfords' personal belongings and how much money it continued to cost them daily. He then asked Gary and Shirley to approach the podium and relate the story in their own words.

They left their chairs and moved to the front of the room. They began to speak, nervously at first, then with more strength and animation in their voices as they looked out over the sympathetic and interested crowd. They recognized compassion in the faces that looked back at them.

Gary and Shirley each explained how, even though they now had temporary work permits, they still couldn't free their possessions from storage. The money they owed was more than they had in their pockets. The bill increased daily, and the problem was continually compounding itself. They were at a point where they didn't know how they were going to satisfy the ever-mounting bill.

They spoke to the gathering for about five minutes, then returned to their seats, a bit uncertain as to what to do next. No one had warned them that this was going to happen. As they sat, Sid's impassioned words made a financial plea on their behalf.

Gary leaned over. "Let's leave for now," he advised Shirley. "We can go to the lounge and have coffee. I don't think we should be here as this goes on." They made their way out of the meeting hall as unobtrusively as possible considering their sudden notoriety.

In the lounge, they couldn't contain their amazement over what had just happened.

"What a wonderful Lord we have, Gary," Shirley's eyes shone with the teary awe she felt. "Most of those people don't even know us, and yet they want to help."

"Yes," Gary squeezed his wife's hand, "Yeshua has indeed provided for all our needs and he never stops doing so, does he?"

They continued to talk quietly, praising God for keeping them in his sight. They were embarrassed and excited. Humbled and happy. Subdued and elated. They were unsure as to what was going on back in the meeting hall, but very certain that the Lord was not only in attendance but presiding over all the proceedings.

Twenty minutes later, a smiling security guard approached them and asked Gary to assist in counting the money that had been collected on their behalf. He agreed and followed to a room with two other persons.

When the counting was completed, Gary's eyes held unshed tears of amazed gratitude. This was more than he or Shirley could have ever prayed for. They had been blessed beyond measure.

In front of him was well in excess of the eighteen thousand shekels needed to get their belongings out of storage. It was his belief that he had just witnessed yet another miracle.

□□□

Shortly after the Shavuot Conference they found themselves

once again experiencing how tenuous was their existence in Israel. Driving to Jerusalem, on their way to a meeting, Gary turned the wheel of their car. Suddenly another car appeared in front of him and he automatically slammed on the brakes. Shirley catapulted forward, fracturing her sternum against the seatbelt. Gary, basically unharmed, tried to make her as comfortable as possible. He worked to soothe her cries while he begged for someone to help his wife.

The police and an emergency vehicle were finally called and Shirley was rushed to Hadassah Hospital. As she lay in a starched white institution bed, any attempt at movement brought about a pain so excruciating that, each shift in position brought her to the brink of unconsciousness.

Gary held her hand tightly. Looking into her clouded eyes, he could sense her piteous cries for help before they came out of her mouth. Yet no medical attention was forthcoming. Doctors checked in on her, nurses walked aimlessly in and out of the room; but when Gary demanded that they do something to care for his wife's injuries, they responded only with vague, unintelligible answers.

In time Shirley was X-rayed, wrapped in surgical tape, placed in a ward and given painkillers. Four days later she was sent home.

Shirley stumbled out of the hospital with Gary supporting most of her weight. She was in tremendous pain. The ride back to their rented home was sheer torture, every bump in the road feeling like a boulder had been dropped on her crushed chest. Gary, too, cringed each time the car rattled, stealing a swift glance at his ailing wife. They couldn't get home quickly enough, yet he couldn't drive any faster.

Once back at their house, trying to resume her daily schedule, Shirley found she couldn't sneeze. She couldn't cough. She certainly couldn't do any housework or gardening. The effort to do much of anything forced her to her knees, and she repeatedly screamed for relief.

"We must pray," Gary told his wife loudly, trying to cut through the sounds of Shirley's agony. "The Lord will help heal you quickly if we only ask it of him." They did, indeed, pray. Then and there, Shirley on her knees, too weak, too hurt to move, and Gary down on the floor beside her.

Within three weeks, after daily repeated prayer, Shirley's chest pains disappeared completely. She was able to throw away the pills that the hospital had given her. Their prayers had been answered.

She had been healed.

□□□

Time passed. Weeks became months. New evidence and arguments were submitted, and as each new piece of evidence required a response, more months passed. Finally the Court put an end to the accumulation of material and announced that they would retire to consider their verdict.

During these months of waiting, the Beresfords awoke each morning on faith. To continue to function in a land which seemed set on shutting them out required that they live not only on their own strength but on the strength of the Lord. Both, by now, had made Israel their physical and emotional home. Yet, by governmental standards, they didn't belong there.

For all practical purposes, the Beresfords were homeless, dependent on the assistance and kindness of others. In some ways, they felt a kinship to Yeshua's disciples who had moved from town to town trying, each in his own way, to do the Lord's work. They, too, experienced a sense of uncertainty in their lives, yet it was not without its rewards.

Finally it was announced that the verdict would be issued on December 25, 1989—Christmas Day in most of the Western World. Gary and many friends showed up at the Supreme Court building at nine in the morning to hear the pronouncement.

Their petition to immigrate to Israel as Jews under the Law of Return had been denied.

In a ninety-page ruling written by Justices Menachem Elon and Aharon Barak, along with Justice Avraham Khalima in agreement, the court determined that the Beresfords were to unequivocally be characterized as "members of another religion," and therefore were ineligible for *oleh* status.

Justice Elon grounded his ruling largely on *halakhah*, Jewish religious law. He did not admit the universality of the saying, "Once a Jew, always a Jew," but said instead that in their long conflict with Christianity, the Jewish people had excluded from their number Jews who believed in Yeshua. Among other things, he wrote, "Messianic Jews attempt to reverse the wheels of history by two thousand years, but the Jewish people has decided during the two thousand years of its history [since then] that Messianic Jews do not belong to the Jewish nation." Period. No room for argument.

Justice Barak's reasoning, unlike Justice Elon's, was not based on Jewish religious law but on a "secular, dynamic, liberal" criterion. He concluded—despite the Dahaf Institute poll—that the Jewish people today were not ready to regard the Beresfords as Jews for the purposes of the Law of Return. But he did not rule out the possibility that at some time in the future, if conditions were different, Messianic Jews could conceivably be regarded as Jews for purposes of the Law of Return.

However, for the present, the Beresfords had lost their cause. They applied for a rehearing before five judges—something like an appeal—but this was denied.

So, still wanting to live in Israel and being unable to do so as Jews under the Law of Return, Gary and Shirley began to pursue a second option. Early in 1990 their lawyer applied on behalf of the Beresfords to the Ministry of the Interior to grant them permanent residency status under the ordinary immigration law applicable to non-Jews, called the Law of Entry.

They just wouldn't stop seeking some sort of legal relief. In response, the Ministry was just as stubbornly unbending. This was evidenced again as the Beresfords once more came up against the hard wall of silence in response to their latest request. Not even a formal denial was voluntarily forthcoming.

Gary and Shirley had long since become accustomed to the Israeli government's silent treatment. Yet, being accustomed to it didn't make it any easier to handle.

Also, it was around this time that Gary and Shirley were introduced to two other Messianic families who had been rejected for entry under the Law of Return because of their Messianic Jewish beliefs. Through the network of people working for a common cause, the Kendalls and Speakmans had learned of the Beresfords and contacted them. Comparing the details of their cases, one could only conclude that the government was systematically trying to ostracize Messianic Jews.

Richard (Ari) Kendall, his wife, Riki, and their four children came to Israel in 1988 from Idaho in the western part of the United States. Ari and Riki had wanted to raise their children as Jews and as Zionists. He is a Jew by birth.

They, too, had applied to the Ministry of the Interior for *oleh* status, and had been denied it because of their belief in Yeshua. After legal maneuvers and pleadings, they found themselves in much the same situation as the Beresfords; they were told to leave the country or face expulsion.

Sidney Speakman wanted to live in Israel in hopes of escaping what he saw as a growing wave of antisemitism. He had discovered this first in his original home of Portland, Oregon, and found the experience confirmed in reports throughout the world. He, his wife and teenage daughter moved to Israel and applied for *oleh* status.

However, the Israeli government was not going to make their move easy. In fact, they seemed determined to thwart the Speakman's efforts at every turn. Their application, too, was denied based on their Messianic faith.

So it was that both families had contacted the Beresfords and their advisors and explained their circumstances. They decided to work together in an attempt to make the public aware of what was happening to Messianic Jews, hoping it would strengthen their cause. As Ari Kendall put it, "If Jewishness is to be determined by personal belief and not by blood relation, where will the investigation of 'Who is a Jew?' end?"

□□□

Some months after the High Court's decision against them, the Beresfords began to hear of new opposition to their efforts to make *aliyah* under the Law of Return. These opponents were not non-Messianic Jews. They were fellow believers! Since the case had implications for Messianic Jews from all over the world, some complained that they had not been consulted before the Beresfords went to court. Others felt the Beresfords were the wrong people to be carrying this burden on behalf of the Messianic Jewish community—they were too new in the faith, too Jewish, too Christian, and so on. Still others seemed to be afraid of rocking the boat with prominent court cases and thereby attracting the attention of would-be persecutors.

Some of these opponents said they represented majority opinion among believers in Israel, but neither they nor those standing with the Beresfords had any real data to support such claims. At one point, at an informal gathering of Israeli congregational leaders a letter was written imploring the Beresfords *not* to ask for a rehearing; but the letter arrived after the rehearing had already been refused. In May, 1990, however, the Messianic Jewish Alliance of America published a full-page advertisement in the International Edition of *The Jerusalem Post*, fully supporting the Beresfords and explaining to the reading public why the High Court's decision was a bad one.

After further discussion of various possibilities, the Beresfords decided to return to the High Court, this time asking them to compel the Ministry of the Interior to at least give them an answer to their request for permanent residence under the Law of Entry—even "no" would be better than silence.

At the same time their lawyer came up with yet another new basis for reconsidering the Beresfords' request for *oleh* status under the Law of Return. After studying the verdict, he concluded that Judge Barak's wording made the criterion for determining whether a person belonged to a "different religion" not the faith of the heart, but his observable acts, particularly any efforts to convince others to adopt the same faith. If it could be shown that the Beresfords were not engaged in such acts, namely, evangelism, he believed that the Court must agree that "conditions" had "changed" and would once again regard the Beresfords as Jews eligible to make *aliyah.*

The Beresfords and their advisors felt a bit uneasy about this strategy. They felt that Mr. Ben-Menashe's suggestion did not seem to take into account the basic biblical principle that faith expresses itself in works. But in the end they agreed to let him pursue the case along these lines—a decision which they later regretted as the unscriptural basis for this approach became more and more evident to all concerned.

Nevertheless, at this stage, the Beresfords were both surprised and pleased when on this new basis Judge Barak granted permission to present a second plea for admission under the Law of Return along with the Beresfords' standing application under the Law of Entry. A spring 1991 date was scheduled.

□□□

This time their belief in Yeshua the Messiah was to be addressed as a legal and religious issue. Was the fact that in one's heart one believed that Yeshua is the Messiah sufficient in itself to place a person in the legal category of "a member of another religion"? If so, the implication would clearly be that one's philosophical views, opinions and beliefs would be subject to the scrutiny of the government. It would, in a sense, imply that Israel was prepared to become a thought-police state.

Mr. Ben-Menashe attempted to use the right words to put these matters of belief into the theological realm where Gary and Shirley and their supporters felt they belonged. If the Court could be made to understand that this was a religious issue, a matter of inward faith and beliefs that could not properly be addressed in a secular legal setting, the Beresfords might win the opportunity to have the entire matter re-examined.

Since the theological issues that had to be addressed touched on points that had been disputed by the Church and the Jewish people for two thousand years, a heavy weight fell upon the shoulders of Mr. Ben-Menashe. But Gary and Shirley put their primary trust in the Lord, that, whatever the outcome, he would be in control and would use it for good.

With a deep sense of awe and a shaky hold on the whirlwind swirling around them, Gary and Shirley were aware that their case was creating legal precedent in Israeli history. The Beresfords were having an impact on the state of Messianic Jewry in Israel. They squared their shoulders for the accompanying responsibilities and difficulties that this fact would unquestioningly carry with it.

□ □ □

The Beresfords' case was heard together with those of the Kendalls and Speakmans; the final arguments were presented in July, 1992. On September 3, 1992, the judges rejected all three families' petitions. In particular, the Beresfords were not permitted to come in under the Law of Return—the Court, unconsciously reflecting Scripture, concluded that the inner faith reveals itself through the works it motivates, so that refraining from performing particular acts cannot be the basis for deciding that a person belongs to a religion. And, continued the Court, the law gives the Ministry of the Interior great discretion in deciding whether to answer positively a petition for permanent residence under the Law of Entry, so that the Ministry of the Interior can virtually never be compelled to grant it.

The final word was that they were eligible for neither citizenship nor residency. Because of the judges' wording in this official decision, Gary and Shirley would not be given the right to a rehearing or any new court date.

Case closed.

The Beresfords had been effectively barred from continuing to pursue their dream through the Israeli court system. Their work permits were no longer applicable; their tourist visas would soon expire.

They had no country to call their home. Their very identity as Jews had been brought into public question. What would they do now?

Chapter Thirteen
BETRAYAL CONTINUES

It was November, 1992. The Beresfords were about out of options. The agony of knowing that they might soon have to leave Israel loomed, day in and day out, on their horizon.

In the midst of this tension, an invitation to the wedding of Shirley's son Steffan arrived. Financially, the two were not in a position even to consider it. Emotionally, though, it was an event Shirley felt she truly needed to attend. They prayed and struggled about what they should do, trying to figure out how to put together enough money to buy Shirley a ticket to Johannesburg.

Reviewing their budget, they realized the money just wasn't there. Soon thereafter, having sadly decided that the trip wasn't feasible, Gary and Shirley received a totally unexpected monetary gift. Overjoyed and flabbergasted, they praised God for his goodness; he had provided the financing for Shirley's trip when all else had failed. Gary decided to stay put and keep a handle on their life in Israel but urged Shirley to go ahead and attend the wedding.

Relationships with her children had been constant sources of both consolation and turmoil, and Shirley felt uncertain as to where this trip might lead. There was an unrest in her heart she didn't understand. Through some intense prayer over her questions, Shirley received the Lord's response in the words of the prophet Isaiah,

> *Arise, shine, for your light has come, and the glory of the Lord has risen upon you.*

This verse would come to have a special meaning for her as events in South Africa unfolded. She would go. No matter what unfolded, Shirley could receive it as God's will.

Her resolve strengthened, Shirley agreed to make the trip. When her eagerly awaited departure date dawned, Gary kissed his wife good-bye at the airport and told her she needn't worry about a thing. "Just enjoy yourself, and savor the time with the family." At her insistence, he promised to let her know the minute they received any further word on their status in Israel.

Arriving at the airport in South Africa following a long, tiring flight, Shirley was energized to see Marlene and her two grandchildren awaiting her. As she came down the ramp, they rushed to embrace her. The children chattered away as she and Marlene collected her luggage and drove to Marlene's home.

Shirley was thrilled to have this time with her family again. Once settled into the house, the children asked to know what presents their grandmother had brought for them from Israel. She dug into her suitcase, laughing, drawing out their anticipation. Slowly, deliberately, she pulled out the trinkets she had lovingly packed away for this very moment.

Eventually she and Marlene were alone for some quiet time.

Driving to the clothing boutique which Marlene managed, they talked awhile about the uncertain immigration situation and then about what was going on in Marlene's life. They also excitedly discussed the upcoming wedding—the colors they would wear, the flowers, what music would be used, how much in love were Steffan and Debbie, his bride-to-be.

Later on that afternoon, back at Marlene's house, Debbie called Shirley and invited her to dinner. She and Steffan would be by soon to pick her up. Dinner went well and there was no sign that anything was amiss. Afterward, Debbie drove her back to Marlene's, and the three women sat down to talk. This conversation gave Shirley the first indication that her presence at this wedding might be a problem.

To her dismay and shock, she was told that not one relative on her side of the family had been invited to the event. In addition, Shirley was not allowed to bring a friend with her. No explanations were offered. When Shirley asked why, her questions were sidestepped.

As she considered these startling announcements, Shirley sighed inwardly. She had hoped that her friend Ari Sorko-Ram, who was in Johannesburg at that very time working on a television project, might escort her to the wedding. Apparently, for some reason, this would not be acceptable.

For the next few days, Shirley held up fairly well under the strain, and continued with her preparations as mother-of-the-groom. Despite a growing uneasiness she didn't completely understand, the days flew by. There was much to attend to. For one thing, she needed to purchase an outfit in the colors Debbie and Steffan had chosen, yet it had to be something that could fit within her meager budget. She prayed she would be able to locate an ensemble fitting for her station, and was rewarded when she came upon a beautiful cream-colored, lace dress. The following day, she visited a milliner's shop for a hat, and then a shoe store. Her outfit was finally complete.

At this point, Shirley knew only that there would be limitations on the guest list. So it was that she found herself one evening, with Marlene at the dress shop, discussing the peculiarities of the impending wedding. Marlene had no insight into what was going on with her brother and his fianceé.

The phone rang. After a few moments, Marlene handed the receiver to her mother. "It's Steffan." She was frowning.

Shirley took the phone. "Mom," the voice on the other end was strained. "I have bad news. The rabbi who is officiating at my wedding..." he stumbled over his words, "he doesn't...well, there's a problem, Mom."

"What's wrong? Tell me." Shirley didn't like Steffan's tone. He sounded guarded and closed to her.

"The rabbi doesn't want you under the *huppa* with me," he blurted out bluntly. "He won't let you give me away."

"But why?!"

"You are a Christian, that's why." Steffan's words were waxen, icy; he could barely restrain his fury. Shirley tried to get her son to talk about the problem, beseeching him to see if there was another way to approach it. She could not imagine being treated like this by her son. It was unthinkable not to be allowed under the wedding canopy.

Steffan would not be deterred. His mission had been given him, and he would fulfill his purpose. The rabbi's mind, he said, was made up. She had only one other choice.

"And what would that be?" Shirley asked. She already knew, with a growing, sick feeling in the pit of her stomach, that she wasn't going to like what she would hear.

"You can stay away from the wedding altogether. But if you do decide to attend—and that decision is yours alone—you must understand that you cannot give me away. And one other thing."

Shirley couldn't speak. The tears were choking her.

"Yes?" she managed.

"Do not discuss any of this during my wedding."

Shirley hung up the phone, now crying uncontrollably. Marlene tried to comfort her, drawing her into a comfortable chair. But Shirley's hurt was so deep, so crushing, that nothing her daughter could say or do would ease the heaviness of her pain. She almost felt as if her son had just died; he seemed that far away from her now.

Time seemed to stop. There was no awareness of minutes or hours. When Shirley was finally able to control her tears, she decided to call on the chief Lubavitch rabbi in Johannesburg. She needed to talk directly to him. Maybe something could be done to fix this worsening situation.

It was only after she had him on the phone for a few minutes that Shirley realized the full, overwhelming sweep of her son's duplicity. Although the rabbi was not interested in a lengthy conversation, he made it quite clear that it had not been at his initiative, but at Steffan's, that Shirley was not wanted under the *huppa.* After a few moments of civilities, she asked the rabbi if she could meet with him in person. He agreed, and an appointment was set for the next day.

Shirley attended the appointment along with Ari Sorko-Ram. As they entered the rabbi's office, they found him polite and courteous, but once she and Ari were settled into their chairs, the rabbi lost no time in making his position and feelings on this issue quite clear.

In even tones, he told Shirley that if she were willing to give up her belief in Yeshua, denounce him right there and then, there would no longer be a problem with her attendance at her son's wedding. She would be allowed under the *huppa* and could partake of the entire array of wedding festivities. She would be warmly welcomed as mother-of-the-groom. He even encouraged her to take some time and consider this option seriously in private, then to return and talk some more after she'd thought about it.

Shirley also needed to have her say, to try and help the rabbi understand why she believed as she did. Surely her beliefs shouldn't affect her involvement in Steffan's wedding. The rabbi listened for awhile, then put up his hand.

"I do not want to hear any of this," he finally exclaimed. "I have no desire to know what you believe. It is of no consequence to me." His voice tolerated no arguments.

Finally Ari spoke up, and Shirley joined in with him. The two began a debate with the determined rabbi considering the possibility that Yeshua is the Jewish Messiah. The talk became heated. Ari and Shirley tried to be as calm as possible. They didn't want to raise their voices in response to the rabbi's raised voice. They didn't want to appear combative in response to the rabbi's defensiveness.

All they wanted from the rabbi was for him to acknowledge that Shirley had the right, as a Jew, to believe as she believed. They also prayed that the rabbi might see the spirit of Yeshua in what they were trying to relate to him.

But after an hour of discussion, Ari and Shirley sadly conceded that the conversation was going nowhere. The rabbi stood. "Enough!" he cried. "I don't ever want to see either of you again. Get out of my office."

Shirley looked at Ari. He nodded. This was non-productive. It was time to leave.

□□□

"I can't go, Marlene. I cannot go to his wedding, not now, after the way he has humiliated me. I will be a laughingstock in front of everyone."

Shirley had just finished talking with Steffan for the second time, bluntly confronting him with what the rabbi had told her. Her son had in turn berated her for making that visit, even daring to taunt her. "I'll bet he ran rings around you, Mother."

Why couldn't she leave well enough alone? he asked loudly, anger punctuating each word. Why did she have to question what he had originally told her? Why did she have to make such a big thing out of her beliefs?

It wouldn't be right for her to give him away. Considering the circumstances, it would be sacrilegious to grant her that most honored spot beneath the *huppa*, next to him as he recited his vows in the beloved, ancient Hebrew. How dare she fly in the face of Jewish tradition! Did it matter *who* had made the decision? It had been made. It was how it was going to be.

Yes, he finally admitted with no remorse whatsoever, it was he, not the rabbi, who barred her from the mother's place next to him under the *huppa*. She had become a traitor to her Jewish heritage, and he'd have no "heretic" defile his wedding ceremony. He reiterated that she could still attend if she so desired, but she was not to participate or to mention this to anyone.

"Think about what you're saying, Mom," Marlene advised after Shirley had hung up and announced that she couldn't take anymore of this. "Think about it very carefully before you decide not to go to his wedding. No matter how he's handling the situation, he is your son. You'll regret it for the rest of your life if you miss his wedding. Especially under these circumstances."

Shirley did think carefully. She realized that to not go would allow Satan, God's adversary, to win this battle. By not showing up at Steffan's wedding, in any capacity, Shirley felt she would permit Satan access to a weak point. It would be a way for him to insinuate himself into her thoughts and emotions. She would not be trusting in God, and this would be the first step on a path of harbored resentment toward her son which, once begun, would be very difficult to reverse.

She had been down that route already, with Javin, and she wouldn't do it again. Her beliefs in Yeshua and his teachings were ones of peace and love; she would not succumb to these hateful influences. She was a mother, and the most vulnerable way to her soul was through her children. Emotions were raw, still she had to have the strength to stand up against the ugliness trying to destroy her.

She would not allow the evil one to have his way.

As Shirley prayed for strength and discernment God answered her. "Arise, shine, for your light has come and the glory of the Lord has risen upon you." In those words Shirley found the strength she needed.

□□□

At the synagogue, Shirley sat with Marlene, her husband, and their two children, in the front row. As the retinue entered, the bride walked in with Steffan and his brother's wife, Tandy, who was taking Shirley's place. Tandy's eyes never met hers; she behaved as if Shirley weren't even there. Seeing this young woman, her own daughter-in-law, treat her so callously, was yet another excruciating turn of the knife Steffan had thrust into her heart.

The rabbi began his speech. Liberally dotted with reminders and admonitions that all in attendance must remain Jewish, must never forget that they were Jewish, Shirley could not miss his point. He drove home over and over again that a Jew had to remain true to his heritage and continue the historically-accepted legacy for the benefit and edification of all future generations.

Shirley felt singled out, as if the speech were given to her and her alone. It felt as if the rabbi were pointing at her and proclaiming for all to hear, "*You* believe in Yeshua as the Messiah. *You* are no longer Jewish."

Her tears were ready to fall. She felt the need to weep until she could weep no more. She had to force herself to hold her head up and compel the tears to wait until she was alone.

The wedding moved into the reception. Her pain continued unabated, accelerating to a crescendo of emotions that threatened to overcome her. Forced to sit by and silently suffer as her eldest son made the wedding speech, Shirley heard her name mentioned almost as an afterthought. She, it would seem, was but a casual, visiting guest. He made note only of the great distance she had traveled to attend.

A smile carefully pasted on her face, Shirley inwardly winced as others also made toasts. Many of them glorified her ex-husband, complimenting him on his wondrous success in raising such a fine son. Not one thing was said about Shirley, Steffan's mother.

It was as if Steffan didn't have, never had, a mother. This was the ultimate betrayal. By denying her her rightful place at his side and avoiding any public comment about her integral part in his life, her son had made painfully clear to their family and friends that he was rejecting his mother and all that she had become. To her, it was also a private denouncement. She had never meant anything to him.

In his eyes she was no longer a Jew, a fact that apparently not only dissolved the future, it erased the past. Yet, through this devastating personal setback, Shirley experienced renewed faith in God, faith sufficient to carry her through whatever life would bring. She no longer feared a day when tranquilizers or other emotional crutches might tempt her as they had in the past. She now knew the truth of Isaiah's words down to the depths of her soul:

> *Arise, shine, for your light has come, and the glory of the Lord has risen upon you.*

Chapter Fourteen

MEDIA INTERVENTION

That same month, Shirley's mother, aged 76 and living in the land as an Israeli citizen, decided to go to the Ministry of the Interior with her own appeal on behalf of her daughter and son-in-law. After scheduling an appointment, she went to the Ministry of the Interior with a friend to personally deliver the letter. In it she pleaded with the government to allow Gary and Shirley *some* sort of status, either permanent residency or citizenship. She requested that they be given this consideration in order for them to continue to reside in the country and help her live out the rest of her life.

Shirley's mother cited her own physical and emotional limitations as the basis for her request—an elderly woman with a heart condition, she was financially unable to live in Israel on her own. She needed Gary and Shirley to remain near her.

Her letter was finally answered, there and then, by a senior official. She, Gary and Shirley were crushed by the cold response. Her request had been flatly denied. Furthermore, if Shirley's mother couldn't accept the answer, she was welcome to move out of Israel and live with her daughter and son-in-law elsewhere. The fact of her own citizenship was baldly ignored.

□□□

Shirley had returned to Israel with a despondent heart. She had not been reconciled with her son; he remained unwilling to have anything to do with her. Knowing that only God could soften Steffan's attitude toward her, Shirley offered her son up to him in prayer. It was time to get back to Gary and to the business of working to secure a legal home in Israel.

Their visas were scheduled to expire in January, four months following the High Court's verdict. They had to decide what they would do. Would they give in to the insistent prodding and leave. Or would they hold their ground and risk the wrath of the Israeli government and any ensuing repercussions?

A few weeks earlier the Beresfords had been contacted by a believer living an Orthodox lifestyle on his small farm in the wilderness, which he had named *Kfar Yeshua*. He had two suggestions. His first, that Gary and Shirley disappear into the desert, was immediately discarded. They felt that this option would be too hard a life for them. The wilderness is at best an unfriendly climate in which to live, especially in the summer when temperatures could rise to one hundred and fifteen degrees.

A second suggestion seemed much more agreeable. He had a friend, a journalist, who worked for the leading Hebrew-language newspaper, *Yediot Acharonot*. They could contact this reporter, explain their story, and ask for help in making their situation known to the general population. In doing so, they might possibly strengthen their position.

Gary and Shirley considered the man's suggestion. Perhaps public opinion could be used to sway the Israeli government. They opted to avail themselves of this new opportunity and arrangements were speedily made for the Beresfords to tell their story to a representative of the media for the first time. They had to travel south to Beersheba for the meeting. Instructions were for them to bring along their *ketubah*—their Jewish marriage certificate—to prove that they had been married in the Jewish faith.

The interview, hours of intense questions, took place on a Sunday. By the following day, Monday, November 9, the article was in the paper with a photo of Gary and Shirley exhibiting the *ketubah.* The following day a second article appeared in the same paper.

Meanwhile, supporters of the Beresfords, Kendalls and Speakmans had suddenly awakened to the fact that in the two months which had elapsed since the High Court's decision, no action had been taken on any front by anyone in the Messianic Jewish community. There was no time to be lost, and a meeting was hastily called, attended by David and Martha Stern, Ari and Shira Sorko-Ram, Barry and Batya Segal and Joe Shulam. Reminding all concerned that God was in full control, the date of the meeting turned out to be the same day as the publication of the article, November 9.

It was decided at this meeting that these people, who had been subjected to years of pressure and disruption in their lives, and finally to two negative verdicts by the High Court, should not simply be abandoned to their fate. At a second meeting the pastors of the families were also present, and at a third meeting the families themselves were invited to join what would be called the Committee for the Three Families.

But long before that third meeting took place, the media of Israel had pounced upon the Beresfords' story and were eagerly engaged in a feeding frenzy. By the middle of December articles and interviews about the Beresfords, Kendalls, and Speakmans had appeared in all the leading Hebrew-language papers as well as the

English-speaking one, and what was truly amazing was that all of them were favorable (except one in an ultra-Orthodox paper). In articles with such titles as *Israeli High Court Rules Against "Messianic Jews," Couple Seeks Support in Fight for Citizenship, Messianics Fight for Recognition in Israel, Can Jews be "for Jesus"?* the families were portrayed as Jews who wanted only to live in the land of their fathers and build up the Jewish state, but who were being irrationally and unjustly prevented from doing so because they believed Yeshua is the Messiah of Israel. The Dahaf Institute poll had suggested there existed a reserve of public support for Messianic Jews, but here was proof.

These newspaper pieces came to the attention of two members of the Knesset (the Israeli legislature), who began taking up the issue from a human rights standpoint and began working on behalf of the three families. As a result they and some of their supporters also became hot property for interviews by magazines, radio and television. After the first articles began appearing in Israel and were subsequently picked up by other journalists outside the country, the Beresford phone rang regularly. Gary and Shirley took turns answering.

One night, Shirley grabbed the ringing phone and, on the other end, was Gary's mother. She was concerned about yet another headline, one she had just read, which boldly stated, "*Jews Face Imprisonment in Israel.*"

"What is going on?! Don't you two think you're taking this Jesus thing too far?"

Shirley's eyes widened and she turned to her husband, who stood nearby. Caught off guard by this sudden onslaught, she was unprepared to respond to her mother-in-law's concern. "Here," she composed herself, "I think you ought to talk to Gary."

Gary's mother continued her tirade as he took the phone. At first almost outraged with worry, it was eventually determined that she had read the article in her Zimbabwean newspaper. Her concern had been brought about by the sudden, alarming notoriety being thrust upon her son and daughter-in-law.

Gary spoke quietly with her for a time. He assured her that he and Shirley were certain of what they were doing. With God on their side, they were prepared to handle anything that came their way. They would not abandon their determination to live out the rest of their lives on Israeli soil.

□□□

Although the Zimbabwe headline had seemed exaggerated, the Beresfords were about to be delivered a jolt of reality concerning the possibility of imprisonment. After Shirley's mother's request had been turned down, it was decided that Gary would personally plead their case with Mr. David Efrati, the Director of Population Registration of the Interior, the most senior official in that government department. It was early December when the meeting was granted. Gary went to the appointment fortified with prayer and with the thought of Shirley and the home they could have, if only this situation might be rectified.

Gary was met by Mr. Efrati and one of his assistants. Forty-five minutes of discussion ensued, most of it in Hebrew, based on the Beresfords' request and the reasoning behind it. Mr. Efrati let Gary talk, and then politely responded that the Ministry of the Interior had already made their policy quite clear. Especially in light of the decision already brought down from the Supreme Court, the Beresfords would not be given any status whatsoever in the land. Basically, they were welcome to just leave.

Gary continued to try and reason with Mr. Efrati. He pointed out that the Supreme Court had denied them citizenship under the Law of Return, but had not stated that they could not become temporary or even permanent residents. Couldn't something be arranged? At this point, Gary and Shirley would settle for anything the government was willing to offer. They simply wanted a secure home.

Mr. Efrati would not bend. Realizing that he was up against an immovable wall, Gary finally rose to leave. Sadly, he looked at the other man and asked, almost conversationally, "Mr. Efrati. What would happen if my wife and I decided not to leave Israel?"

There was a long, pregnant pause. Gary refused to look away. When he received his answer, it was the hardest blow yet in a long line of unending insults.

"Mr. Beresford," Mr. Efrati stated slowly, "I would be compelled to sign a deportation order. You and your wife would be picked up by the police and be imprisoned until such time that we could put you on a plane to some country outside of Israel."

Gary's hand was on the door. "I see, Mr. Efrati, I see. Well, if that's the way it's going to be, that's the way it's going to be." He took a deep breath. "You know, Mr. Efrati, this is like being in Germany before the war." The official did not answer, but Gary noted the stern, disturbed flash of anger that passed over the official's usually implacable face. Then Gary walked out of the office to the stairwell leading from the building. He knew that his exterior appearance to the official had been one of strength and determination; inside, he was petrified at the ramifications of this latest bout with the Israeli government.

Gary had no immediate answers. He uttered a quick prayer as the outside air hit him hard in the face. The only one who did have answers was the God of Abraham, Isaac, and Jacob. God had deemed it right that all Jewish people would live in the land of Israel, according to his prophetic word. God would see this through.

□□□

Gary and Shirley constantly encountered interested people, some supporting and some denouncing their cause. It became an almost-hourly occurrence for the phone to ring with yet another reporter asking for an interview. On the street the Beresfords were often approached by people who had read about them . Their mailbox was flooded with letters endorsing one or the other side of the argument.

When they attended their first meeting of the Committee for the Three Families, it was determined that in addition to taking public action, it was now necessary to make an effort to unite the community of Messianic congregations behind the effort. By this point, many Jewish and non-Jewish believers in the land were confused and ignorant of what was happening and even of what the court decisions meant. Some individuals and leaders stood solidly with the Beresfords in their need; others were disturbed and distressed over them.

The committee planned meetings in Jaffa to explain what was behind their efforts and to dispel any circulating untruths. All interested members of the believing Messianic congregations within Israel were invited to come and thresh out whatever points concerned them.

Two full meetings were required to handle all the questions and the worries over whether or not this effort would further or hinder the Messianic movement in Israel. By the time the second meeting had ended, those present experienced the sought-for unity and a decision was reached that the Messianic congregations represented there would formally and publicly stand behind the Beresfords, the Kendalls, and the Speakmans.

As the Beresfords' case became more and more public, many people wrote letters to the government on their behalf. One such letter came from Shirley's son Javin, the one who had originally turned them in to the Jewish agency. Javin, though no longer embracing Yeshua, had softened and had written to the President of Israel requesting leniency on behalf of his mother and stepfather. Paul, Shirley's youngest son, wrote a similar letter. And just as surprisingly, an overwhelming number of strangers, many of them people who had heard of the problem through the ongoing media attention, also wrote in support.

At the same time the Beresfords were facing deportation,

another situation of national importance faced Israel. As a result, the media were forced to work overtime. Some four hundred members of the Hamas, the Muslim Fundamentalist movement, were causing major political and social upheaval. Efforts to force them out of the country, a move which the public overwhelmingly supported, were being met with warnings of recrimination from the Arab world. Should the Hamas deportation go through, retaliation would take place. Political tempers were heating up on both sides.

As reporters interviewed Gary and Shirley, they bent one ear to the radio to hear the minute-by-minute reports of what was happening with Hamas. The Beresford talks were often interrupted by late-breaking news on Hamas. The Beresford deportation suddenly became second in importance to the immediate need to expel Hamas terrorists from Israel, a matter which threatened national security.

It was natural for the media to contrast the potential deportation of the Beresfords with the deportation of the Hamas activists. Hamas threatened the very fabric of Israeli society, whereas the Beresfords posed no threat to anyone. Any comparison was ludicrous. Their only "crime" was their religious belief.

The kind, gentle manner of Gary and Shirley Beresford had already won over many of the reporters. The hassles Gary and Shirley were receiving at the hands of the government were viewed as less and less acceptable. Even unreasonable.

Shirley was an attractive, grandmotherly woman with a head of strawberry blonde hair. She spent most of her time gardening, taking care of her modest home, and tending to countless stray animals; she couldn't help but play nurse to any wounded dog or cat. It was detestable to her—and she made vocal note of it—that the national animal society in Israel paid little attention to the orphaned animals walking their streets.

Gary Beresford had taken on assorted redecorating, carpentry and odd-repair jobs. Also, some while earlier, he had been given a scholarship by the Center for the Study of Early Christianity to work on a Master's Degree program, with the Dead Sea Scrolls and the Jewish origins of Christianity as his central focus.

His impish sense of humor, and Shirley's gentle and compassionate nature had garnered them many friends on both sides of the religious argument. The Beresfords, agreeable, likable people, were being portrayed that way.

With their sudden popularity in the Israeli limelight as the couple most unlikely to cause an insurrection, Gary and Shirley felt relieved of the threat of immediate deportation. Still, they remained under the ongoing, possibility that eventually, at the whim of the government, they might have to leave their beloved Israel. As each new day dawned, they were aware that the deportation effort could begin anew. They were still in danger of literally being forced out at a moment's notice, driven from the country to which they had become totally committed.

The entire situation was publicly likened to the beginning of another Holocaust. If Jews were being persecuted throughout the world because they were Jews, where else were they to go but to Israel? Israel was a country built on the principle that Jews from all over would always be welcome there. Many felt that they were, indeed, facing exclusion from other countries and societies because of their birthright. Yet, in Israel, some of these same Jews were becoming victims of reverse discrimination.

The Beresfords were touted as the most vocal Messianics in recent history trying to stay in Israel without persecution. Yet the voices of the Speakmans and Kendalls also demonstrated that Gary and Shirley weren't the only ones. One article went so far as to state, "If the Beresfords...had lived in Europe in Nazi times, they would have ended up in the gas chambers together with their Jewish brothers and sisters" (Quote from *Svenskka Daqbladet*, 2/93). The article did not explicitly ask, but left hanging in the air, the unspoken question, "If they would have died as Jews in Auschwitz, why can't they live as Jews in Israel?"

□□□

Gary and Shirley discovered that they had American supporters and, to their surprise and gratitude, learned that these Americans were not only interested in voicing their opinion, but also willing to step in and get involved.

The existence of these people clearly hit home through a call from Micha Ashkenazi, an Israeli tour guide and well-known archaeologist. The Beresfords had met Micha briefly a few years earlier. He explained that there were Messianic Jews in the States who wanted to offer their services, and he had been asked to be their contact person. After hearing the entire story told personally by the Beresfords, he was astounded.

"This is ridiculous!" His words exploded. He made it known that while he wasn't a Messianic believer, he felt that every Jew deserved the right to believe as he or she wished to believe. He vowed to do whatever he could to help the Beresfords to legally remain in Israel.

"You are both full Jews. Not only are your mothers Jewish, but your fathers are also Jewish. You have family in Israel, as well as children who serve in the Israeli army. How can the government possibly deny you citizenship?!" he asked incredulously.

Micha wasted no time beginning his campaign within existing committees, hoping to bring the situation into an even larger arena. He also set to work with Dr. Stern and formed a new committee consisting of Micha and various members of Israeli society outraged by the government's attitude towards the Beresfords and the other two families. This committee was to be composed of Jews who *didn't* believe in Yeshua as Messiah.

At the same time a second group of people calling themselves the "Bridging Committee" was formed from the Committee of the Three Families to coordinate action. Dr. Stern, who classified the Beresford case as "the biggest deportation scandal..." acted as chairman, and the Sorko-Rams worked directly with him.

Two press conferences were called in late January, the first in Tel Aviv and the other in Jerusalem. A number of print reporters made an appearance in Tel Aviv, along with a photographer and a "Voice of Israel" radio reporter.

Gary took on the task of personally inviting members of the international press to the second conference. The committees informed the local press, so the event was expected to draw a crowd.

On the day of the Jerusalem conference, Gary and Shirley arrived early, prayerfully prepared for whatever the Lord would have in store for them. They felt in every fiber of their being that this would be a turning point. Their life's work was sealed. It had become their mission to bring the name of Yeshua to the Jewish people in particular, and the world at large, no matter what obstacles would be thrown in their way. They wanted the world to know that the Jewish religion is not destroyed by acceptance of Yeshua as Messiah.

The turnout was spectacular. Twenty-five reporters came from international newspapers and from other media outlets in many countries—Finland, New Zealand, Australia, Sweden, China, and more. *The New York Times, Newsweek, The Los Angeles Times,* and *The Washington Post* all sent representatives.

Most of the reporters were Jewish. They asked pointed, probing questions indicating a sincere desire to discover the driving force behind the Beresfords' determination to live in Israel. This, it appeared, was not simply a story for them, but an issue which provoked intense, personal questions.

One journalist, in particular, seemed overly affected. An Orthodox Jew, he worked for a leading news magazine in Jerusalem. Following the conference, this man contacted the Beresfords, asking numerous follow-up questions. His desire, it was clear, was to get to the core of their beliefs. He was openly interested, even eager, and didn't close himself off when the Beresfords discussed their love for Yeshua.

At the end of their second interview, he remarked that he could deeply feel their sincerity. In his opinion, they had become so much more, rather than less, absorbed in Judaism *expressly* because of their belief in Yeshua. The Beresfords, he believed, truly saw the Messiah as the core of all Judaism.

□□□

Through the committees' open forums, through the gathering support of Israel's Messianic community as well as through personal interviews, the Beresfords, Speakmans, and Kendalls escalated their efforts. It was imperative that they develop a unity that could stand public exposure.

People soon became aware of the Jewish believers as a very cohesive group. Both the believing and non-believing communities looked with intense interest at this tight, organized front. Operating on the principle of strength in numbers, the committees and their growing numbers decided to seize on the increasing exposure by holding a solidarity rally. They selected a site opposite the Prime Minister's office in Jerusalem, inviting Israel's entire Messianic Jewish community. Three Knesset members, concerned with the human rights aspect of the cases, were also respectfully requested to attend.

Because of the teachings of the Torah, the Israeli work week begins on Sunday and ends on Friday evening. With this in mind, the rally was held on a Sunday. Participants gathered on a hill overlooking the Prime Minister's office in the Knesset. Three hundred Israeli believers showed up to make their presence felt.

They were determined that Messianic believers should be given as fair an opportunity as any other Jews to live in Israel, and to live there as the Jews they are. The demonstrators were not willing to accept the way Gary and Shirley and the others were being treated.

Commuters drove by. Some leaned out of automobile windows, trying to get a glimpse of what was going on, waving and exhibiting a supportive victory sign to picketers as they realized what the demonstration was about. On their way to work and going about their daily business, many walked past the placards which had statements such as "Once a Jew, Always a Jew," "Stop the Deportation of Jews," and "Let My People Stay." Many Israelis paused to listen as the demonstrators gave impassioned, imploring speeches.

One protester told *The Jerusalem Post*, "It is humiliating that [they] deport Messianic Jews from Israel at a time when the state brings in refugees (2/22/93)."

An article written by Cordelia Edvardson and translated into English from the Swedish daily paper *Svenskka Daqbladet* said, "If someone were to believe his or her pooch were actually the Messiah, such a person would doubtless be considered somewhat eccentric. But the idea would hardly be grounds for deportation. It is the name of Jesus which creates goose bumps up and down the backs of the religiously zealous in the Ministry of the Interior."

The Bosnians were Muslims, certainly not Jewish. Yet the government had allowed many to settle in Israel. In years past the government had permitted over a hundred Vietnamese "boat people" to become permanent residents; they too were not Jewish. Moreover, the government had also let several thousand so-called "Black Hebrews" remain in the land, who, despite what they call themselves, are not of Jewish descent.

In contrast to the Beresfords' plight, these groups were granted legal status in Israel, despite the variety of political and religious views they held. There seemed to be only one overriding difference in the cases—the Messianics were Jews who called upon Yeshua.

Several hundred members of Israel's believing community participated in the rally. Micha Ashkenazi, in the midst of the energized crowd made up of believing and non-believing Jews and gentiles, proclaimed loudly, "As a tour guide whose income depends mostly on Christians, I see a drop in my income because of this stupid decision. Do we really need another deportation scandal?"

Another group of protesters who shared this particular location on that day were a group from the Golan Heights who were protesting giving up that area as part of Israel. They had brought several tons of snow from Mt. Hermon to Jerusalem, piling it outside the Prime Minister's office. The protesters wanted it made clear that they would never be willing to give up the Golan in the name of "peace," and certainly not by edict of the government.

Most of the Golan Heights protesters were Orthodox Jews and, although they didn't understand how any Jew could believe in Yeshua as the Messiah, they didn't condemn the believers' cause. Quite the opposite; they welcomed the comforting fellowship of their fellow-protesters. Each group had created its own spirited atmosphere; the Golan Heights protesters embraced the Beresfords and their group as equally deserving of public attention.

After the two groups spent time together in the same public area, they shared their personal religious beliefs. Gary and Shirley were invited to visit for a weekend with one of them, an Orthodox lady. She explained that she intellectually understood what the Beresfords and their group believed and it didn't matter to her. She had no problem with them. Quite simply, she enjoyed their company.

This woman didn't pretend to accept what the Messianics professed, yet she in no way felt threatened by their emotions and love for Yeshua. That was how they felt and that was their prerogative. Their differing views would not get in the way of them becoming friends. She was attracted to their personalities and admired their single-minded determination.

That alliance, as well as the extensive amount of time Gary and Shirley spent sharing their hearts with the protesters from the Golan Heights, helped to allay the fears of many other non-believing Jews. It proved that the opposition against Gary and Shirley was not an across-the-country, personal opposition. Instead, it seemed to have a political origin. It also gave further credibility to the results described in Dr. Stern's earlier "man-on-the-street" poll.

The more the Beresfords met with and talked to individuals

on both sides, the more people began to understand that Gary and Shirley did not intend to bring a different religion to the land of Israel. In fact that was the last thing they wanted.

On the contrary. They believed that the only true religion of the Jewish people *was* Judaism. Changing this was never a part of what they intended. What they prayed for was the chance to help make the Jewish life even more Jewish by including the Jewish Messiah, Yeshua.

□□□

The publicity surrounding the Beresfords had intensified the discussion not only in non-believing Jewish sectors, but in the Messianic community as well. Some claimed that Messianic Jews had no right, spiritually, to demand acceptance by the non-believing Jewish community. They cited Hebrews 13:12–13, "Yeshua suffered death outside the gate.... Therefore, let us go out to him who is outside the camp and share his disgrace." Others quoted Yeshua's more general prescription, "Turn the other cheek," urging that Messianic Jews should give up court fights, publicity and other such activities. Scripture calls believers to a passive role, they asserted; we should *expect* rejection by those who do not share our faith. The Beresfords, therefore, should simply pack up and leave. But few holding this opinion were themselves packing their own bags!

Some in the Messianic community felt it was wrong to air Messianic Jews' problems in the international media, reasoning that it would only provide an occasion for more Israel-bashing. Better, they said, to accept some persecution and the attendant consequences of restricted immigration than to be held accountable for projecting a bad image of Israel. Clearly, they felt, this was a matter of weighing values: Israel's justice vs. Israel's image. None of the three families or their supporters would voluntarily publicize negative aspects of Israeli society to the international community without very good reason. They understood the international community's bias against Israel was already strong; people seemed far too eager to expose Israel's every flaw while ignoring the more egregious transgressions of Israel's neighbors. But those who concluded that securing justice for Messianic Jews was more important than boosting Israel's international image stood with the Beresfords and not against them. With a heavy heart they decided to accept a degree of international outcry against their own beloved country, Israel, believing that their cause justified such a position.

Believers found themselves in a quandary, tossed between the two opinions. Since the government had clearly denounced them, and since their beliefs went against the grain of widely-accepted Jewish views, then perhaps they had no right to force themselves into the public eye. Going through the court system to stake their claim may have been pushing too hard. Controversy and dissension within the Messianic community rose to the surface. Many wondered aloud, "Do Messianic Jews really qualify for the same rights as other Jews?"

And if the Israeli courts, cornered into denouncing the entire Messianic community, had rejected them as Jews, did the Messianics have any right to go farther? Should they quietly leave the country; or should they stay and fight, as the Beresfords were doing?

Those siding with the Beresfords claimed that if Messianic Jews were being persecuted in Israel based solely on their belief that Yeshua is the Messiah, then those Messianic Jews who sided with the persecutors were abetting this persecution, indeed, facilitating it, by not standing up to be counted.

□□□

The pot was now beginning to boil—and not only in Israel. The questions and continuing attention brought out the media all over again, both national and international, coming to the

Beresfords' defense in ever-widening circles. Both *Time* and *Newsweek* published feature articles. The British Broadcasting Corporation put together a documentary on the plight of Messianic Jews in Israel which featured Gary and Shirley. Cable News Network's two hundred million viewers were treated to six showings of a three-minute report on the Messianic Jews in Israel. Throughout the world, people, believers and non-believers alike, began to ask the question, "Are Messianic Jews being persecuted in Israel solely because they believe that Jesus is the Messiah?"

The Dahaf Survey, commissioned by Dr. Stern had originally been conducted in 1988, before they went to court; now it was taken out and re-examined. The results were as pertinent as they'd been before. Eighty-two percent of the Israeli public holding opinions (seventy-eight per cent of the public as a whole), from Orthodox to secular, believed that anyone who lived as a Jew and who identified with the Jews of Israel, deserved to be granted Israeli citizenship.

If only the court would agree.

Chapter Fifteen
ONWARD TO WIN THE PRIZE

Public attention was focused on the Israeli government and what was beginning to be seen around the world as an international human rights incident. What would happen to the Beresfords and their compatriots? This was a question many people in Israel, and elsewhere, were asking. They were holding the Israeli government accountable to answer.

So it came as a surprise when the Ministry of the Interior flatly upheld their previous decisions even in the face of the February 21 demonstration. Still the Beresfords were not even granted a tourist visa. They had already been visa-less and therefore living illegally in the land for a month.

Meanwhile, much negative attention became focused on a small but most powerful faction of the Israeli government, the ultra-Orthodox *Shas* party. They were against the Messianic

Jews. Yet, despite this sudden wave of unappealing attention, they would not budge.

The Ministry of the Interior was run by Aryeh Deri, head of *Shas*. One important point was becoming increasingly obvious to everyone working for the Beresfords' cause. This battle would be next to impossible to win within traditional, legal parameters, unless someone of great political power intervened, someone as influential as Deri.

At that time, it seemed almost irrelevant that Deri had been under investigation for over a year on fraud charges, or that a close associate of his had just been jailed for similar offenses. Deri had a strong grip on national and political power; someone had to challenge him if any progress was to be made.

Three members of the Knesset had cast their lots solidly with Gary and Shirley: Benny Temkin, Yossi Katz, and Naomi Chazan. Benny Temkin, Chairman of the Knesset's Human Rights Caucus, invited Shirley and Gary to testify before the Caucus. They were asked to explain in detail their point of view, and what had happened to them as a result of that view being made public.

Due to their testimony and the strenuous efforts of Mr. Temkin and his colleagues, Gary and Shirley and the other two families were granted three extra months to remain in Israel on tourist visas. These Knesset members made it quite clear that they did not share the Beresfords' religious beliefs; however, they indicated that they would not let that fact stop them from standing with Gary and Shirley. Their support, they explained, was based solely on the principles of basic human rights and the dignity of the Jewish tradition.

Another consideration in the Beresfords' favor was the fact that, according to the original rulings in their case, the High Court had *not* specifically stated that Gary and Shirley had to be deported. Instead, the Court had left this up to the discretion of the Ministry of the Interior.

Thus, it was the Ministry of the Interior alone—specifically the decision of Aryeh Deri—which had ruled not only to deny the

Messianics' request for permanent residence under the Law of Entry, but to demand their expulsion as well. In direct contrast, this same Ministry had granted permanent residence under the Law of Entry to dozens of Bosnian Muslims, many Buddhists from Vietnam, and a countless variety of non-Jews from around the world.

The media offered to speculate on this irony. They posed the question to the Ministry personnel. "We get thousands of requests a year from non-Jews wanting to live here," stated David Efrati, the Ministry's Director of Population Administration. He was the official in charge of the Beresford case. In an interview with *The Jerusalem Report*, a biweekly English news magazine, he stated, "If we give in [to them] we will have to give in to many others."

It was suggested that perhaps the Ministry of the Interior might be willing to retreat just a bit from their hard-line stance concerning the Messianics in order to let the controversy die down. Chances were, the general population would question the Ministry's judgment in these two matters.

□□□

It was early 1993. Though they had been granted a short extension on their tourist visas, Gary and Shirley were not fooled. They knew the ways of the Ministry of the Interior well enough by now. They were fairly certain that Deri and his personnel had likely acquiesced to the extension simply to give the Beresfords time to pack their belongings and finally—for good—leave Israel. This time maybe, just maybe, the reasoning seemed to go, the Beresfords might quietly disappear.

After all, hadn't the Ministry office made themselves very clear, not only with their decision, but with their public statements?

□□□

With all the attention the Beresfords and their plight received, few in Israel did not know of this human rights and religious issue. Most people found themselves choosing sides. But more than that, Israelis began to seriously and vocally join the debate which was at the heart of the Beresford case:

Who really *was* the Messiah?

Then, at just this moment, from the other side of the world, something happened which further highlighted this burning issue. During the time that the Hamas deportations were made public, and as the Messianic solidarity groups were demonstrating outside the Prime Minister's office, an old rabbi in Brooklyn, New York, thousands of miles away, was declared by his zealous followers to be the Messiah.

This was the same international movement, the Lubavitch Hasidim, from which Javin had sought counsel just before turning Gary and Shirley in as believers. Even though Javin no longer identified with them and had since asked his mother's forgiveness, it seemed that this group, through Steffan and now inadvertently through this rabbi, their leader, would continue to somehow figure in their lives.

The aged, lined face of Rabbi Menachem Mendel Schneerson appeared everywhere, on posters and placards. His followers chanted his name. They boldly demanded that all world Jewry recognize him as the Messiah. The cry reached Israel and the Israelis began taking note.

As a people, Jews had been looking for the true Messiah for millennia. Most seemed to feel that each claimant deserved at least a fair hearing. The Beresford case had thrust the claim of Yeshua before the people in his ancient land. Now Israel was faced with an announcement that the *real* Messiah was an American, in Brooklyn, a man who had never once set foot in the promised land.

Again the question was raised: Who *is* the true Messiah? Was it this American rabbi, born in Russia, or was it Yeshua, who was born in Bethlehem as Micah 5:1–2 prophesied.

Cartoons came out in the newspapers. Comedy skits were

performed on television. Rabbi Schneerson from Brooklyn, New York, was pitted against Yeshua of Bethlehem. Under pictures of the ailing, ninety year-old Schneerson were the words, "Blessed is He who comes, King Messiah!" The people themselves were left to make the choice.

Most of the media carried the item in a satirical fashion; if one or the other had to be selected, at least Yeshua had definitely been born and lived in Israel. To many, the "contest" became a game. A joke.

Knowing that she and Gary were at the very core of this intense debate, Shirley watched as an Israeli TV commentator weighed the pros and cons of each "candidate" for Messiah. She smiled serenely at her TV screen as she absently petted *Yehudah*—Judah—one of her cats, named for the area in which she lived. The other, cat *Shomrona*, named for Shomrom (Hebrew for Samaria) lay curled obliviously at her feet.

She looked skyward, addressing her words to Yeshua, the real Messiah.

"Your name is being heard throughout this country and the world," Shirley whispered, her voice shivering with excitement and joy. "You're being discussed and debated with rising fervor. They may not believe now, but at least they're talking about you. Thank you, Lord, for allowing Gary and me to be part of it."

□□□

In the meantime, the Beresfords' friends in the Knesset, working overtime in an effort to keep them in the country permanently, devised a legislative maneuver not previously attempted. The Human Rights Caucus, now in full swing, created a bill which, if adopted, would amend the Law of Entry; then they sponsored the bill in the Knesset.

Under this proposed amendment, anyone could be automatically eligible for permanent residency if he had a first-degree relative (a parent, brother, sister, or child) with Israeli citizenship acquired under the Law of Return, or a first-degree relative who had served in the Israeli Defense Forces.

Although the bill would not grant them citizenship, through it Gary and Shirley, and others in similar situations, would have the option to stay in the country indefinitely as permanent residents. The Beresfords fit both stated criteria—Shirley's sons served in the IDF, and she and Gary had relatives with Israeli citizenship obtained through the Law of Return.

Still living as a couple without a country, they set about waiting, all over again, their ever-impending fate which was in the hands of the Israeli government. No deportation order had been issued against them. If they could just hold on long enough, there was the possibility that a new option would be made available to them.

This national battle had started out as a couple's simple desire to be with their people in their land, and undergirding that desire was their personal belief that the Lord required it of them. Now it had become an ongoing, seemingly-never-ending struggle, an international media event, and a moral, legal, and spiritual focus of world debate.

The Beresfords had now become public representatives of the Messianic Jewish movement; in a relatively short period of time, their lives had been changed forever. They were being seen as a test case for the entire worldwide Messianic Jewish community—a group that exceeds 100,000 in the United States alone. How would the outcome of this case now and in the future legally and spiritually relate to the State of Israel?

The opposition—both inside and outside of government—felt that if this unassuming husband and wife won their case, Israel would be inundated by a never-ending influx of Messianic Jews. The very core of traditional Jewish belief might even be threatened. These people were no more than "a wayward cult" in the eyes of those non-believers. Israel would never again be the same.

Yet, Israel had undergone ongoing change since first becoming a state in 1948. It had fought bitterly and bravely for a difficult independence. It continued to fight for boundaries and governing rights to the surrounding areas. Israel had always been a country very obviously built on the richness, ideals, and beliefs of its diverse population.

It had also been a country for centuries fought over and built on the ancient conflict between believers in Yeshua and non-believers. There had always been those who did not agree that Yeshua owned a very specific place next to God. There had also been those who did believe, Jews and gentiles alike. Pro-Yeshua and anti-Yeshua factions had pulled at Israel since the days he himself had walked the earth. Why should now be any different?

The Beresfords found themselves in a position directly in the middle of this tug-of-war. Their comfortable life in Zimbabwe was gone forever. Whether or not Israel ever accepted them as residents or as citizens, they would, from this point on, work to proclaim the name of Yeshua as the Jewish Messiah—indeed, the Messiah of the world.

They could never go back to being unassuming people who lived their beliefs behind closed doors. For Gary and Shirley, being Jewish was not simply a religion to practice haphazardly, it was an identity. Th*eir* identity. The Beresfords stood in the midst of a battle. Did they qualify for the same rights as Jews who held onto the long-standing, more accepted tenets of Judaism, most importantly, that Yeshua was *not* the Messiah?

Had the "promised land" *really* been promised to *all* Jews?

According to conventional beliefs, Judaism traditionally judged one who claimed to be the Messiah on the criterion of world peace. It was thought that if the "claimant" didn't bring about such a peace with his arrival, he could not be the Messiah. True, Yeshua had preached peace and love; yet the world, since his arrival and death, had never known overall peace. Based upon this single test, many Jews could not embrace Yeshua as Messiah.

To the standard-definition Jews, they were ridiculed for their faith in Yeshua.

It was absolutely impossible for Gary and Shirley to accept that faith in Yeshua could ever turn a Jew into a non-Jew. So many other Jews held a varied array of religious beliefs, yet none had received recrimination. None had been denied citizenship. None had forfeited Jewish identity. Why should the Messianic Jews, why should the Beresfords, be different?

If it went against the very core of traditional Judaism to proclaim a differing spiritual viewpoint, why were other groups accepted? Why had followers of other supposed "Messiahs" been merely brushed off as mistaken? Why hadn't Rabbi Schneerson's followers, too, been threatened with deportation when they proclaimed their rabbi to be the Messiah? Rabbi Akiva, in the second century C.E., had falsely proclaimed Simon Bar Kochba the Messiah. Yet his memory continues to be venerated by Jews. Why the inconsistency?

And, now, today, why are Jews who believe in yoga, Transcendental Meditation, Scientology, or Hare Krishna granted residency and citizenship? Jews who have adopted the practices of Hinduism, Confucianism, New Age philosophies, reincarnation, Satanism, Bahaism, and a plethora of other spiritual expressions do not find themselves living lives of persecution.

Why? Why are *they* still accepted as Jews in the eyes of the Israeli government and the world at large, while Jews who embrace Yeshua—a Jew from birth who lived and died as a Jew—are ostracized and condemned?

An unrelated newspaper column written by Dr. Hyman S. Frank in the May 22, 1987, issue of *The Jerusalem Post* included the statement, "...self-preservation...justifies even violation of secular or religious law." It seemed to the Beresfords—and others in the Messianic community—that self-preservation had become the issue. There seemed to be a political force, bent on preserving itself, driving the attempt to publicly humiliate Gary and Shirley.

Why was it so hard to understand and accept that, for the Beresfords, being Jewish was *their* entire identity, just as could be said for any Jew. Just as it had been for Yeshua, from the day he was born, till the day he died.

A special brand had been placed upon each Jew by God himself. No one on earth could take this from the Beresfords, any more than they could remove it from Yeshua, or from any other Jew. No one.

The Knesset and the Ministry of the Interior of Israel might rule in their favor, or rule against them. Either way, the Beresfords would never give up their work to see that all Jews—Messianic or non-Messianic—were allowed to return to the land of Israel. And to remain there forever.

Above all, one fact could not be changed. Yeshua was and would continue to be the Messiah. For Jews. For all the world. For all eternity.

Chapter Sixteen

EPILOGUE

Close to seven-and-one-half years have passed since we arrived in Israel. Much has been said by both Israeli government institutions and by Jewish followers of Yeshua. Some, as you have read, have stood with us through the tough times and the easy times, whilst others have opposed us.

We have never seen ourselves as better or worse than others who follow the Messiah. We have, however, realized that nothing has ever been established without those people who believe in what they are doing — whether the Maccabees or the martyrs of the Messianic faith.

The modern history of Israel is filled with the names of courageous men and women who, despite persecution—both in the limited-immigration policies of the British mandate as well as from militant Arabs—were willing to stand firm. This proved to be a triumph for the Word of God and a victory for Zionist visionaries both religious and secular.

Likewise today, Jews who believe in Yeshua and have not renounced their Jewish heritage must have the right to return to their God-given, God-promised land. The arguments that faith in Yeshua is not Jewish, or that it undermines Judaism, do not hold water.

Most of Israeli society, well over seventy-five per cent, do not regard themselves as Jewishly religious. Cults are openly followed throughout Israel. Hedonism and secularism are two more factors which gnaw away at the very core of the Jewish religion. Our desire is to follow the Jewish teachings of Yeshua—rabbi, dare we say it, redeemer, a native-born Israeli. His teachings are indigenous to biblical Judaism and are truly consistent with all that is and ever was historically Jewish. Contrast this with imported religious practices, with cults, with Messianic pretenders who have never set foot in Israel, let alone been born here.

We have continued to live our lives as Jews, observant to the best of our abilities, never running from the religion we were born into, but immersing ourselves in the blessings of practicing our Judaism in the land of the Jews. Yet, we have never denied our following of the Messiah and his teachings.

Looking back at statements made by judges in both our court cases, we cannot help but see the ridiculous situation that has persisted. Clearly, the judiciary has made statements that do not fit in with the thinking of the majority in Israel. This becomes more and more obvious as months roll by.

In our first case, one of the judges stated that when a Jew converts to Islam (the Moslem religion), Judaism will not see that person as Jewish any longer. But this, once again, has turned out to be incorrect. During the tragic terrorist bombing of a bus in Afula in the spring of 1994, a young woman was killed who, shortly before her death had converted to Islam from Judaism and married a Moslem. When it came time for her to be buried, it was decided, with the kind and thoughtful permission of her husband, to bury her in the Jewish cemetery. This, from a Jewish religious point of view, is a privilege reserved *only* for Jews. Thus, despite the judge's pronouncement, according to Jewish religious law she was still considered Jewish!

What does the future hold? We are not seers. What we know is that we have made Israel our home, even though we live from tourist visa to tourist visa, always without a working permit. We live on the outskirts of Jerusalem, and for the time being this is our home.

For the first time in seven years we spent the Rosh haShanah (New Year) and the Yom Kippur (Day of Atonement) in the United States, with friends in Florida. We became all the more convinced that we belong in Israel. Even though the synagogue services were rewarding spiritually, there is something about being in Israel for the High Holy Days that cannot be expressed or experienced outside the land.

Over the years, and especially during the past few months, a number of Jewish followers of Yeshua have had their applications for immigration turned down by the Ministry of the Interior. We urge them to have the courage and persistence of their Jewish predecessors who, following the trauma of World War II and the Holocaust, and facing the might of triumphant Britain, nevertheless determined to come to the land featured in Jewish prayer for 1,800 years—and succeeded.

This is a time when bureaucrats and politicians are proclaiming the dawn of a new era; when "peace" is bring struck with terrorists and with those who openly state that their religion seeks the demise of the Jewish people and of Israel. Refusing citizenship or even permanent residency to a group seen by the world as a persecuted stream within Judaism is not a wise policy for Israel.

In conclusion and in retrospect, the vast majority of Israel's Jewish followers of Yeshua have a track record of being loyal, honest, law-abiding citizens, serving in the defense forces with dignity and strength of conviction. Jewish believers in Israel will continue serving our fellow Jews and Israeli society.

Over the years of our struggles there have been those who have stood with us and are still standing at our side. Among them are the Sorko-Rams, the Stern family, Joseph Shulam, the Powlisons, Hefzibah Congregation and the Pearlmutters. They have shared with us the good times and the bad. We also thank Micha Ashkenazi, the non-believer—as well as most of the people of Israel. We have not mentioned the names of all those throughout the world who have stood and still stand with us, especially so many dear friends in the U.S.A. But in deference to wisdom, since we don't wish to see problems arise for them when they, in their time, seek to fulfill the call to the land of Israel, we shall let them remain nameless.

The last word to you shall be that of Rav Sha'ul (Paul) of Tarsus, the most maligned and misunderstood *shaliach* (apostle), from his letter to the congregation in Rome, chapter 9, verses 1–5, quoted from Dr. David Stern's *Jewish New Testament* translation (Jerusalem, Israel and Clarksville, Maryland 1989):

> *I am speaking the truth—as one who belongs to the Messiah, I do not lie; and also bearing witness is my conscience, governed by the* Ruach HaKodesh [Holy Spirit]*: my grief is so great, the pain in my heart so constant, that I could wish myself actually under God's curse and separated from the Messiah, if it would help my brothers, my own flesh and blood, the people of Israel! They were made God's children, the* Sh'khinah [the manifest glorious presence of God] *has been with them, the covenants are theirs, likewise the giving of the* Torah, *the Temple service and the promises; the Patriarchs are theirs; and from them, as far as his physical descent is concerned, came the Messiah, who is over all. Praised be* Adonai [the Lord, Jehovah] *for ever! Amen.*

—Gary & Shirley Beresford

Appendix
MESSIANIC JEWISH *ALIYAH* IN THE PAST THREE DECADES

In an effort to present the reader with an overview of the issue of Messianic Jewish *aliyah*, returning to the homeland as full-fledged Jews, we asked Dr. David Stern for permission to include two articles he wrote as an Appendix. These articles form the most thorough summary of the *aliyah* issue since the 1960's.

—*The Publisher*

□□□

THE BERESFORD CASE AND ISRAELI PUBLIC OPINION ABOUT MESSIANIC JEWISH *ALIYAH*

by David H. Stern, Ph.D.

On December 25, 1989 the Israel High Court of Justice delivered its negative verdict on the petition of Messianic Jews Shirley and Gary Beresford to be allowed to make *aliyah* (immigrate to Israel) as Jews under the Law of Return.

In January 1988 Israel's equivalent of the Gallup Poll, the Dahaf Research Institute, directed by Mina Tzemach, Ph.D. (Psychology, Yale), surveyed a demographically balanced sample of 1,189 Israeli Jews on the question of whether Messianic Jews should have the right to make *aliyah* under the Law of Return.

Because I initiated and supervised this opinion poll and also have been involved with the Beresfords' lawyer, Yosef Ben-Menashe, in preparing several aspects of their case, I have been asked to write an article on how the Beresford case judges related to the Dahaf survey. But to make the article more widely usable I want first to review the history of the Law of Return in relation to Messianic Jews and then to present the main findings of the Dahaf Survey. After this I will address the topic I'm to write about.

1. History of the Law of Return in Relation to Messianic Jews

The Law of Return, passed in 1950, allowing any Jew anywhere in the world to make *aliyah* and become a citizen, was one of the first bills passed by the new State of Israel. It made a national policy of the ancient Jewish hope to live once again in the Land. In this law a Jew was defined as "anyone born to a Jewish mother or converted to Judaism." On its face, Messianic Jews were included.

In 1962 the High Court of Justice ruled against Daniel Rufeysen, a Jewish Carmelite monk who tried to make *aliyah*, calling himself a Jew by nationality and a Roman Catholic by religion. The court said that even though "Brother Daniel" had a Jewish mother and was thus *halakhically* Jewish, nevertheless the secular State of Israel was not bound by *halakhah* (Jewish religious law) and could make its own determination of who is a Jew for the purpose of its Law of Return. The court made use of a "man-on-the street" criterion: Shmulik in Jerusalem's Mahane-Yehuda shuk and Itzik on Dizengoff Street in Tel Aviv would not consider Brother Daniel, wearing a brown monk's robe and a cross around his neck, a fellow Jew. Therefore, said the court, he isn't one.

In 1970 the court, in the only case ever decided by all nine justices, decided that the population registry law allowed Benjamin Shalit (a non-Messianic Jew) to register his son as a Jew, even though his wife, the son's mother, was a gentile. This provoked a government crisis in which that law was changed; and at the same time the Law of Return, to take account of the Brother Daniel case, was also changed by adding to its definition of a Jew the following phrase: "who is not a member of another religion and did not voluntarily change his religion." The subsequent Dorflinger and Beresford cases have revolved around this addition.

Eileen (Esther) Dorflinger was born to a Jewish mother and claimed that although she believed in Jesus she had not changed her religion but had come to know the Jewish Messiah. She had been baptized but said her baptism had been not into a church but into the Body of the Messiah. In 1978 the High Court of

Justice ruled against her.

First of all, evidence was produced that she had indeed been baptized "into a church" — her name was found on the membership roll, and its present pastor confirmed this. For some reason Esther did not produce countervailing evidence from the former pastor, who had in fact baptized her with the specific understanding that she was being baptized into the Body of the Messiah and not into any institution. Second, and more importantly, although Esther produced Scriptural and historical evidence that Yeshua fulfills the *Tanakh*'s promises concerning the Messiah and that the early believers in him remained Jews, the court concluded otherwise in her case. No Jew today, it ruled, can believe that Jesus is God or that God is a trinity. Also, although the early believers were indeed Jews, the clock can no longer be turned back to the first century — there has been an unbridgeable parting of the ways between Christianity and Judaism. In short, some very bad ad hoc theologizing was done from the bench.

Thus the Brother Daniel case produced a practical, secular criterion: if the man in the street thinks a born Jew isn't Jewish, he isn't. But the Dorflinger case produced theological criteria involving biblical interpretation, a person's private thoughts and allegedly unchangeable historical developments.

In 1986 Gary and Shirley Beresford came from South Africa and Zimbabwe to make *aliyah* but were refused entry by the Department of the Interior because of their faith. They took their case to court, and it soon arrived for decision by the High Court of Justice.

Upon looking over the material submitted before the hearing to Yosef Ben-Menashe by the lawyer for the Department of the Interior, I found that the old "man-on-the-street" criterion of the Brother Daniel case was being resurrected. I asked myself why we should be bound by the conventional wisdom which assumes that the Israeli "man in the street" is opposed to Messianic Jewish *aliyah*. It occurred to me that so long as no one inquired of the real man in the street, he could be depicted as having any opinion convenient for one's argument; but if a research institute above reproach in regard to both scientific methodological competence and religious/ideological bias would conduct a proper survey of public opinion, this could no longer happen. Thus was born the Dahaf Survey, whose results, I am pleased to say, overwhelmingly refute the conventional wisdom. For it is evident that the majority of the Israeli Jewish public, whether religious, traditional or secular, welcomes Messianic Jewish *aliyah* under the Law of Return.

2. The Dahaf Survey of Israeli Jewish Public Opinion Concerning Messianic Jewish *Aliyah*

The interviews were conducted face-to-face in the homes of the interviewees during the week of January 17–24, 1988. The interviewees were presented with the following statement as background information:

> *The Law of Return determines that every Jew may immigrate to the Land of Israel. The Law defines "Jew" as anyone born of a Jewish mother or converted to Judaism, who does not belong to another religion and who did not voluntarily "change his religion." This definition allows for different interpretations.*

Then the interviewees were asked the following question about ten categories of possible immigrants:

> *In your opinion, does the person described as follows have the right to receive an immigrant's visa under the Law of Return?*

Table 1 presents the findings.

TABLE 1: (See Note B)

INTERVIEWEES' REACTIONS CONCERNING THE RIGHT OF PEOPLE IN VARIOUS CATEGORIES TO RECEIVE AN IMMIGRANT'S VISA UNDER THE LAW OF RETURN

(NOTE: The data are presented not in the order in which the questions were asked the interviewees, but in order of the percentage voting in favor of the right to receive an immigrant's visa under the Law of Return. The numbers at the left of the table show the order in which the questions were asked.)

THE QUESTIONS, AND ORDER IN WHICH THE QUESTIONS WERE PRESENTED	HAS RIGHT	DOES NOT HAVE RIGHT	NO RESPONSE	TOTAL
1. A person born to a Jewish mother, who does not believe in the existence of God. (See Note B)	83	13	4	100
10. A person born to a Jewish mother, who is faithful to the State of Israel, pays his taxes to the State, serves in the army, celebrates the Jewish holidays, keeps commandments from Israel's tradition, feels that he is a Jew, and believes that Yeshua is the Messiah, but was not baptized into Christianity. (See Note C)	78	17	5	100
4. A person born to a Jewish mother, who does not believe that the Torah was inspired by God. (See Note B)	73	22	5	100
5. A person born to a Jewish mother, who believes that both Torah and New Testament are inspired by God.	68	27	5	100
7. A person born to a Jewish mother, who was baptized in the framework of a Messianic Jewish congregation.	63	32	5	100
8. A person born to a Jewish mother, who believes that Yeshua is the Messiah, considers and feels himself a Jew, and was baptized in the framework of a Messianic Jewish congregation.	61	34	5	100
3. A person born to a Jewish mother, who believes that Yeshua is the Messiah.	61	35	4	100
2. A person born to a Jewish mother, who is a member of Hare Krishna, Scientology or similar cult. (See Note B)	61	35	4	100
9. A person born to a Jewish mother, who believes that Yeshua is the Messiah, considers and feels himself both a Jew and a Christian, and was baptized in the framework of a Christian church.	54	41	5	100
6. A person born to a Jewish mother, who was baptized in the framework of a Christian church.	49	46	5	100

Notes to Table 1

Note A

Statistically, there is a 95% probability that the percentage figures based on the 1,189-person sample, the figures shown in this report, are not more than 2.5 percentage points away from the true percentage figures for the Israeli Jewish population of 3,630,000.

Note B

Questions 1, 2 and 4 are "control questions" relating to groups other than Messianic Jews. They provide a context or background standard with which to compare opinions about Messianic Jews as revealed by the other seven questions.

Note C

I must admit that this question was badly worded, because the phrase, "but was not baptized into Christianity," could be interpreted by the interviewee to mean either (1) "was indeed baptized (as the New Testament requires) but was not thereby transferred out of the Jewish community or Judaism into the religion known as Christianity," or (2) "was not baptized at all." This ambiguity makes the question unclear and may cloud the conclusions to be drawn from it.

From Table I can be deduced the following:

a. An absolute majority of the public (more than 50%) favors granting an immigrant's visa under the Law of Return to all the categories, except someone "born to a Jewish mother and baptized in the framework of a Christian church." And even in this case, a majority of those expressing an opinion favors granting the visa, 49% to 46%.

b. The category, of those defined in the survey, which the highest percentage of interviewees (83%) supports granting the right to an immigrant's visa under the Law of Return is "persons born to a Jewish mother, who do not believe in the existence of God." Actually, I was amazed that as many as 13% opposed *aliyah* for

Jewish atheists and agnostics. However, the 83% figure serves as a benchmark against which the other categories can be measured.

c. From the order of the categories as presented in Table I it is obvious that there exist groups of categories which have different "support rates" on the part of the interviewees. The highest support rates were for Jews who do not believe in God at all (83%), and persons born to a Jewish mother who are loyal to the state of Israel, keep Jewish tradition, identify with the Jewish people and believe that Yeshua is the Messiah (78%). The lowest support rates were for Jews baptized in the framework of a Christian church (49% and 54%). Inbetween were support rates for Jews who belong to cults or believe in Yeshua as the Messiah (61–63%).

d. According to Mina Tzemach, the gap between the 78% support rate for the Messianic Jew whose loyalty to his people and the state is made explicit and the 61% support rate for the prototype described briefly as "a person born to a Jewish mother, who believes that Yeshua is the Messiah" could be due to either of the following reasons: (1) the other characteristics of the person—"faithful to the State of Israel, pays his taxes to the state, serves in the army," etc.—outweigh the fact that he believes in the Messiahship of Yeshua; or (2) the many other factors mentioned in the question obscure the element of his faith in Yeshua.

My own explanation is that when a member of the public is asked whether he would favor allowing on *aliyah* someone born to a Jewish mother who believes in Yeshua, he wants reassurance that such a person is not a traitor to his people but remains Jewish, as evidenced by Jewish lifestyle, self-identification with the Jewish people and loyalty to the Jewish state. This also helps explain the differential support rates when question 7 is compared with question 9 and when question 6 is compared with question 7.

The interviewees in the survey also identified themselves as religious (*dati*), traditional (*masorati*) or secular (*chiloni*). Table II presents differential responses of these three groups to the ten questions.

Table 2:

Percentage Of Religious, Traditional and Secular Interviewees Supporting The Right Of People In Various Categories To Have The Right To An Immigrant's Visa Under the Law of Return

QUESTIONS, AND ORDER IN WHICH THE QUESTIONS WERE PRESENTED		RELI-GIOUS	TRADI-TIONAL	SECULAR
1.	A person born to a Jewish mother, who does not believe in the existence of God.	78	79	89
10.	A person born to a Jewish mother, who is faithful to the State of Israel, pays his taxes to the State, serves in the army, celebrates the Jewish holidays, keeps commandments from Israel's tradition, feels that he is a Jew, and believes that Yeshua is the Messiah, but was not baptized into Christianity.	77	75	82
4.	A person born to a Jewish mother, who does not believe that the Torah was inspired by God. (see Note B.)	71	68	78
5.	A person born to a Jewish mother, who believes that both the Torah and the New Testament are inspired by God.	57	67	74
7.	A person born to a Jewish mother, who was baptized in the framework of a Messianic Jewish congregation.	55	59	69
8.	A person born to a Jewish mother, who believes that Yeshua is the Messiah, considers and feels himself a Jew, and was baptized in the framework of a Messianic Jewish congregation.	50	57	69
3.	A person born to a Jewish mother, who believes that Yeshua is the Messiah.	50	54	69
2.	A person born to a Jewish mother, who is a member of Hare Krishna, Scientology or a similar cult. (See Note B.)	57	54	68
9.	A person born to a Jewish mother, who believes that Yeshua is the Messiah, considers and feels himself both a Jew and a Christian, and was baptized in the framework of a Christian church.	26	48	63
6.	A person born to a Jewish mother, who was baptized in the framework of a Christian church.	27	43	57

Note D

36 Interviewees did not place themselves in any religious category. Also, only 12% of the sample self-identified as religious, while 20% of the population does. The general results reported in Table I incorporate a weighting of the sample data to reflect the true proportions in the population.

From Table 2 can be deduced that although the support rates of religious Jews are lower than of secular Jews, the more so as evidence for Christian identity becomes stronger, nevertheless more than a quarter of them would be willing to grant immigrant status to Jews baptized in a Christian church. More remarkably, a majority (50–57%) of religious Jews would grant the right to immigrate under the Law of Return to Jews who believe Yeshua is the Messiah and/or have been baptized in a Messianic Jewish congregational framework (questions 3, 5, 7 and 8). And most remarkably, no less than 77% of the religious hold the view that a Messianic Jew who is loyal to the state, identifies with his Jewish people and keeps Jewish tradition should be allowed to make *aliyah*; this is only 5 points below the 82% rate for the secular.

3. The Beresford Case Judges and the Dahaf Survey.

The Beresford case was heard before Judge Menahem Elon, an Orthodox Jew who served as deputy president; Aharon Barak, a secular Jew; and A. Chalima, an Oriental Jew who is probably traditional in outlook. In the end, all three judges voted to reject the Beresford petition. The first two wrote opinions, while Judge Chalima, who has since resigned from the bench, concurred with the decision.

The first session was on February 4, 1988, and I will never forget it. The results of the Dahaf poll had been raced to the court to be included in the file only a couple of days earlier. Uzi Fogelman, the lawyer for the Interior Department, was only a few minutes into his initial presentation when he brought up the Brother Daniel case and its "man-in-the street" criterion of Jewishness. Yosef Ben-Menashe then did something extraordinary. He interrupted Mr. Fogelman to ask, "Have you judges seen the Dahaf Survey?" — They fumbled through their papers to find it and began to read. A high point in my life was seeing Judge Barak's jaw drop in amazement when he discovered that 61% of the Israeli Jewish public would allow a Jew who believes in Jesus to make *aliyah.* His world was turned upside down; no longer could it be said that the Israeli man in the street cannot accept a Messianic Jew as a Jew for purposes of the Law of Return.

Or could it? It was our turn to be amazed when we read the verdict. Menahem Elon, as might be expected of a religious Jew, paid no attention to the Brother Daniel precedent but used exclusively the Dorflinger precedents, so that mention of the Dahaf Survey in his opinion was made only in passing:

> *Mr. Ben-Menashe, the petitioners' learned representative, who sought to convince us that from a Jewish viewpoint the petitioners are acceptable as Jews entitled to an immigrant's visa under the Law of Return, submitted to us a public-opinion poll that had been ordered by the petitioners and been conducted by the Dahaf Research Institute, headed by Dr. Mina Tzemach. According to the results of the poll, so the petitioners' representative contends, the opinion of 78% of those polled is that a person such as the petitioners should be entitled to immigrate to Israel under the provisions of the Law of Return, as against 17% who voiced an opposite view and 5% who did not respond.*
>
> *Only marginal significance attaches to this poll, and the only reason we mention its submission is out of respect for the petitioners' representatives, who made every effort to argue for this poll's importance in deciding the question confronting us. I have been young and am almost old, and I have*

neither seen nor heard of a court reaching a decision based on a public-opinion poll. That is generally useful for supplying different social and political needs, but it does not meet the requirements presented by the law for the submission of evidence or for its acceptance. But even in essence the poll does not provide an answer to the question before us. Mr. Fogelman has rightly pointed to various faults in the poll: the information presented to the pollees was inexact, and the question presented on the basis of this inexact information was in the nature of seeking an opinion and interpretation of a juridical nature from pollees not qualified therefor. Further inexactitudes thus occurred therein. It is inconceivable that such a poll should serve the court as material upon which to decide so fundamental issue as the one before us.

Judge Elon did not specify what "faults" Mr. Fogelman pointed out or what "further inexactitudes...occurred," and I do not know them from other sources, so there is no more I can say about it. However, since Judge Elon did not use the man-in-the-street criterion at all in his own opinion but based it entirely on historical, theological and *halakhic* criteria as he perceives them, his view is, as he says, that "only marginal significance attaches to this poll."

Our greatest disappointment was reserved for Judge Barak, who voted with the majority. Although, in contrast to Judge Elon, he developed a secular, dynamic liberal basis for defining who is a member of another religion, so that in principle the court could reverse itself in the future, he nevertheless managed to base his opinion on the very notion — that the man in the street cannot accept a Messianic Jew as a Jew for purposes of the Law of Return — which I suppose the Dahaf Survey had relegated to the realm of superstition. He wrote:

What is the secular substance of the expression, "and is not a member of another religion"? Meseems it is the same substance that gives the expression 'and is not a member of another religion' a significance according with the general purpose of making the State of Israel the state of the Jewish people and not that of those who, because of their other religion, are not perceived—in the secular perception I touched upon [earlier in the opinion]—*as members of the Jewish people. To that end it is vital that their other religion be their effective religion, to which they would see themselves bound in their daily life, and it is vital that this effective link not accord with the secular perception of a person's being Jewish. An example thereof is provided by "Brother Daniel", whose affair was considered in the Rufeysen case. A person born to a Jewish mother, who is yet a Christian priest, is a "member of another religion", since, according to our secular perception, by virtue of his being a priest he ceased being Jewish...*

I pointed out that the secular-liberal perception is a dynamic one. It changes with the Jewish people's passage through its history. When employing the criteria of this perception, let us employ neither criteria that obtained in the past but have undergone change, nor criteria that have not yet materialized and are still future. We should employ those criteria that have gained currency at present in the Jewish people's perception,...regarding which there is national agreement....

The judge will get to know this national awareness through study of all the data before him: Jewish history, national independence and the nation's survival in its land. He will draw upon the "sources of the social consciousness of the people" within whom he dwells (Landau), and he will consider the people's "system of national life" (Agranat). Indeed, the judge is part of his people. He may at times be in an ivory tower, but it is an ivory tower in the hills of Jerusalem and not on Greek Olympus. The Judge is alert to what is happening

> *among the people. He knows the nation's history, its perceptions in matters of state and religion, and its yearning for deliverance, its hope for absorption of its immigrants and its heartbeats. He studies its literature and poetry, both ancient and modern, and the various researches. Meseems that in this framework there can be no fault in conducting a poll that would properly reflect the present-day feelings of "the Jew in the street". A poll conducted scientifically may serve —and does actually serve in the social sciences—as an instrument for gathering information about the social perceptions obtaining in a particular society at a given time. Indeed, if we are seeking the approach in the present attitude of 'the Jew in the street', I see nothing wrong in a properly conducted poll. It is, of course, not decisive, and should occupy its rightful place alongside other data regarding the present secular perception. All these would be taken into account by the court when giving expression to said secular-liberal perception as to a person's being a "member of another religion" with reference to the Law of Return.*

Thus Judge Barak managed to refer to "a poll that would properly reflect the present-day feelings of 'the Jew in the street'" without revealing any awareness of the Dahaf Survey at all! And no wonder! For had he referred to the Dahaf Survey he would have had to acknowledge that the criterion which has "gained currency at present in the Jewish people's perception,...regarding which there is national agreement," is nothing else than a pronounced and broadly based willingness of the Israeli Jewish public to grant Messianic Jews immigrant's visas as Jews under the Law of Return.

4. THE FUTURE OF MESSIANIC JEWISH *ALIYAH*

If the Beresford case returns for re-hearing before five justices of the High Court (they would be Elon, Barak and three others), we can anticipate another year to three years' delay before a final decision is handed down. But whether the case is re-heard or not, certain processes have already been set in motion. For if the Beresfords finally win, it can be expected that certain elements of Israeli society, including, but not limited to, some of the *dati'im* [Orthodox], will press the Knesset to pass a law that would clearly and specifically exclude Messianic Jews from acceptability as Jews under the Law of Return, so that we Messianic Jews will be forced to express our opposition publicly. On the other hand, if the Beresfords finally lose, it will be up to us to transfer the battle from the courts to the arena of politics and public relations (which of course does not imply that I exclude the arena of prayer, for we should pray about everything).

One positive function of the Dahaf Survey should be to reassure us that we do have friends. In effect, the majority of Jewish Israelis believe our cause is just. And many of these will take a public stand on our behalf. For there are in Israel Jews who call themselves secular but do in fact have a religion, namely civil rights. These people are our allies, and they are not few.

Moreover, although we Messianic Jews have always been underdogs, we are now becoming publicly recognized underdogs. This is often a key element in developing the public relations aspects of a social movement, including slogans that catch the public's attention. We are Israel's *refuseniks*. We would have died as Jews in Auschwitz, so why can't we live as Jews in Israel?

Finally, as a result of "going public" I expect that a whole new approach to evangelism will open up to us. Instead of having to force the Gospel on people uninterested in it, we will find people coming to us. Their awareness of injustice being done to underdogs will naturally lead them to ask, "Why don't they want you to be here?" And that is a question we will be more than glad to answer!

MESSIANIC JEWISH *ALIYAH* — UPDATE SINCE THE BERESFORD DECISION OF 1989

by David H. Stern, Ph.D. , Jerusalem

Shortly after the December 25, 1989, decision of Israel's High Court of Justice ruling Messianic Jews ineligible to make *aliyah* under the Law of Return, I was asked to write an article called "The Beresford Case and Israeli Public Opinion About Messianic Jewish *Aliyah*"; it appeared in issue no. 20 of the LCJE Bulletin (May 1990). Now I have been asked to bring the matter up to date. And there is much to tell.

But before I do, I must say something about Israel's two immigration laws, the Law of Return and the Law of Entry. The Law of Return is Israel's unique law allowing both Jews and the non-Jewish descendants of a Jewish father or a Jewish grandparent to make *aliyah* (immigrate) to Israel and quickly receive citizenship. This law defines as a Jew anyone who was born to a Jewish mother or who converted to Judaism, but who is not a member of another religion or voluntarily converted to another religion. The Law of Entry is a standard-type immigration law under which any non-Jew may apply for immigration; in practice few are admitted.

1. FIVE CASES

In May the Messianic Jewish Alliance of America broke new ground by publishing in the International Edition of *The Jerusalem Post* a full-page advertisement opposing the High Court of Justice's verdict and explaining to readers why Messianic Jews are still Jews. By this time, in the aftermath of what I will call the First Beresford Case (Beresford I), Joseph Ben-Menashe, the lawyer in Beresford I, was busy with five Messianic Jewish families who had been refused *aliyah.*

The Ministry of the Interior had rejected four other families — the Kendalls, Speakmans, Marlowes and Lewins. All were prepared to fight their cases to the High Court of Justice if necessary.

But in time the Lewins left. And the Ministry of the Interior eventually allowed the Marlowes to remain in Israel because their *oleh* visas, granting residence under the Law of Return, had been issued prior to Beresford I, the court case which for the first time defined Messianic Jews as "members of another religion" and thus ineligible for *oleh* status.

The Kendall parents were ineligible according to Beresford I, but their four minor children would, at majority, become eligible to make *aliyah* under the Law of Return as the descendants of Jewish grandparents who had not changed their religion. Ben-Menashe attempted to gain permanent residence under the Law of Entry for the parents too, on the ground that they should be the guardians of their own children.

The Speakman situation was more confused. Linda Speakman, whose parents are Jewish, was ineligible by Beresford I. Sydney's mother was gentile and his father a Jewish Christian, so by *halakhah* (Jewish religious law) and by the Law of Return Sidney is not Jewish. But the father's parents were understood to have been Jewish and not Christian, so Sidney should have made *aliyah* under the Law of Return as the non-Jewish grandson of Jewish grandparents. But for various reasons involving misunderstandings all around, this did not happen; and it took the High Court of Justice to set matters back on track.

The Beresfords too got back in the act. First they petitioned for a rehearing of Beresford I by five High Court justices, a procedure somewhat like appeal permitted where important issues are at stake. A letter from a number of Israel congregation elders requested them to desist from this step on the ground that a decision by five judges would further damage the cause of Messianic Jewish *aliyah*. This letter never reached the Beresfords, but the matter became moot when President Shamgar of the High Court of Justice turned down their request.

They then developed a new case based on the reasoning of High Court Judge Aharon Barak in Beresford I. While the Orthodox Jew Menahem Elon's reasoning in that case, drawing on his understanding of halakhah, had excluded the possibility that a Messianic Jew could ever be considered a Jew for purposes of the Law of Return, Judge Barak had employed a "dynamic, liberal" criterion for determining who is a Jew, in which he had allowed that under changed conditions Messianic Jews might become eligible.

To my mind Barak meant that someday judges might perceive the general social climate among Israelis to be compatible with accepting Messianic Jews as Jews under the Law of Return and would then reverse Beresford I. But Ben-Menashe took "changed conditions" to mean that if the Beresfords' own conditions changed enough, in ways conforming to Barak's criteria laid down in his decision, then the Beresfords personally ought to be admitted as Jews under the Law of Return.

The Beresfords' participation in the Ramat HaSharon Messianic Jewish congregation led by Ari and Shira Sorko-Ram had been a key element in showing that they were "members of another religion", but now they were no longer members of it and had in fact moved elsewhere. This was part of their "changed conditions".

Also Ben-Menashe concluded that Barak's criteria for belonging to another religion consisted of a list of acts, not beliefs. More specifically, the proscribed acts were those which served to win others to join one's religion. He advised the Beresfords to refrain from such acts, that is, from street evangelism, attending congregation meetings, and the like. With other Jewish believers I was present in his office when this approach was laid out, and to my shame I admit that I went along with it at the time. Clearly this strategy is inconsistent with Ya'akov (James) 2:14–26, which says, "Faith without works is dead." Restricting oneself to becoming a "closet believer" without deeds openly expressing one's belief is, to my now cleared mind, sin. All of us who let this happen are guilty, and we have acknowledged our sin publicly to the Body of the Messiah in Israel.

2. Beresford II — The Decision

In the summer of 1992 the High Court of Justice heard the cases of the Beresfords, Kendalls and Speakmans together; and on September 3, 1992, the verdict was published. All three families were refused entry, both under the Law of Return and under the Law of Entry — with the following exceptions: the Kendall children and the Speakman child would become eligible at majority for entry under the Law of Return as the non-Jewish descendants of Jewish grandparents; and if Sidney Speakman could provide adequate evidence that his mother was gentile (!) and a parent of his father Jewish, he too could enter in the same way under the Law of Return.

The opinion of Judge Shoshana Netanyahu, who chaired the panel, dealt with the issues directly concerning the three families. She quickly zeroed in on the "faith/works" issue mentioned above:

> *Religion is a matter of faith which is and will be expressed in acts...Judge Barak did not see in* [the Beresfords' membership in congregations of Messianic Jews and the dissemination of the matter of their religion] *a fundamental element of the test, pursuant to which would be determined whether they are members of another religion, but, rather, an expression, an indication of their faith. The secrets of the heart, the thoughts and faith of a person, no one can know, unless he gives them external expression. The faith which is in the heart can be given external expression in acts, as it was in the activities of the petitioners, but it can also be expressed and revealed in other ways, such as in writing and verbally.*
>
> *It is inconceivable that a test determining the religious status of a person according to criteria can be subject to change from day to day. It is inconceivable that the status of a person as a Jew for the purposes of the Law of Return would be determined according to a changeable test of activity (or, perhaps,*

also its intensity?), so that he will act or cease to act whenever he wishes to do so. Today he believes in another religion but does not engage in any activity on its behalf, and he would be considered a Jew. Tomorrow he will return to his activity and be a member of another religion, and so on and so forth, heaven forbid.

[T]*his is not what Judge Barak intended in his test...*

The Beresfords did not establish that the change, according to their argument, which occurred in their actions, is a sincere change which resulted from an inner conviction.

In short, Judge Netanyahu understood the substance of Ya'akov 2:14–26 much better than we did.

Judge Y. Maltz concurred without comment; and Judge David Cheshin in his opinion commented on the substantial latitude granted by the legislature (the Knesset) to the Ministry of the Interior in granting visas under the Law of Entry. Basically, the Ministry is not required to give any reason for refusing a visa under this law (and this is common in many nations' immigration laws); yet there are limits to the Ministry's freedom of action, which the Judge enumerates and reviews.

On another topic raised above Judge Netanyahu wrote,

This attempt to build [the rights of the parents] *upon the rights of minor children, which are conditioned on the declaration of their desire to settle in Israel, will not succeed... The place of the minor is with his parents. Wherever they settle, he will settle, and not vice-versa. A minor is dependent of his parents. Parents are not dependent upon him.*

However, concerning the matter of non-Jewish descendants of a Jewish father or grandparent, what she wrote has possibly disturbing implications. Section 4A(a) of the Law of Return provides, in part,

> *The rights of a Jew under this law and the rights of an immigrant under the Nationality Law 5712–1952, as well as the rights of an immigrant under any other enactment, are also vested in a child and grandchild of a Jew; except for a person who has been a Jew and has voluntarily changed his religion.*

She comments,

> *This Section does not deal with a Jew but with someone who is not a Jew. The legislators thereof declared concerning it that it was enacted to resolve the 'problem of granting rights...to those who are not Jews but have a connection with the Jewish nation by means of a spouse, parent, grandfather or grandmother who were Jews; and with the hope that in this manner the commandment would be fulfilled,* "[Your] *sons will return to their own border* [i.e., country]," *and that those who were detached, taken out of the Jewish nation, would, by their coming to Israel, find the way to return to the bosom of their fathers, would rejoin the Jewish nation according to the definition, and would convert and become part of it..."—from the words of the Chairman of the Constitution, Legislation and Juridical Committee, 2nd and 3rd readings Knesset Speeches 57 [5730], pp. 1118–1119.*

In other words, Section 4A(a) offers a Jewish environment to gentiles with Jewish roots only so that they will convert to Judaism. Whether this citation from the Knesset debate reflects the majority view or only the view of the chairman at the time of the legislation was passed is not clear to me. I had thought, myself, that Section 4A(a) was made part of the Law of Return for a very different reason, namely, to offer refuge to anyone in the world with even one Jewish grandparent, since the Nazis systematically sent all such to the ovens and gas chambers. I have not done the research necessary to find out whether my view or Judge Netanyahu's is the correct one. But if her understanding of the legislature's purpose is right, one can imagine her opinion becoming ground for restricting entry under this Section only to gentiles showing interest in converting to Judaism.

These and other points in the decision are important in understanding the whole picture of how the High Court of Justice has related to Messianic Jews. But, apart from my remarks above, I don't see much new ground being broken in this case. The "Brother Daniel", Dorflinger and Beresford I cases described in my earlier article created the landmarks produced by Israel's judicial system. Beresford II largely reaffirmed and solidified what had been said in Beresford I.

3. Since Beresford II: A Resistant Ministry and Good Publicity

Following the publication of the Beresford II verdict in September 1992 the Ministry of the Interior gave the three families until January 19, 1993 to leave Israel. For the first two months nothing happened—nobody left, nobody engaged in organized discussion of the case: nothing. I suppose we were all in a state of shock or depression that what we had feared had come upon us.

But on November 9 two things occurred. My wife Martha and I had a meeting in our home with Ari and Shira Sorko-Ram, Joseph Shulam and Barry and Batya Segal—all people who, like us, had been involved for years with these court cases. In this and subsequent meetings, which were expanded to include the three families and persons in pastoral relationship with them, we reached three conclusions:

1. It would shame the Body of the Messiah to permit these three families to be expelled from the Land of Israel without our doing all in our power to prevent it. So we must act to this end.
2. We seven who managed the court cases made serious mistakes,

which we must acknowledge. Not only were we sinful and foolish in allowing the faith-without-the-works strategy in Beresford II, but we did less than we should have to maintain open lines of communication with Israel believers who were opposed to the court cases for various reasons. Yeshua prayed for our unity (Yochanan/John 17:20–23), and while overall unity in the Body may be too broad a goal for our small forces, we can certainly do everything from our side to prevent needless divisions that result from failure in communication and lack of understanding.

3. The High Court of Justice has spoken and has defined Messianic Jews as "members of another religion" ineligible to immigrate under the Law of Return as Jews. Nothing further can be expected from the courts. The future of Messianic Jewish *aliyah* now depends on changing the wording of the Law of Return. Accomplishing this will involve a shift of our activity from the courts to the arena of politics, publicity and public relations. As of the time of writing, we have not, as a group, made a commitment to pursue this goal. Our commitment now is to a much narrower goal, insuring that the three families can stay in the Land. But this is not a bad thing: we are learning the ropes in these new areas.

The other thing that happened on November 9 was the publication in a Hebrew newspaper of a sizeable article highly favorable to these families. Within days, Israel's reporters had begun a feeding frenzy, seeking out the three families and those of us who could provide background information on Messianic Jewish *aliyah* and on Messianic Judaism generally. It became evident that not only were these Messianic Jewish families a hot news item, but the reportage was highly favorable—they were being presented as Jews who love Israel, on whom Israel was perpetrating an injustice or at least an unkindness, not as apostates or enemies.

Moreover, we noticed a number of factors we could never have orchestrated. While born Jews were being refused admission,

Bosnian Muslims were being offered refuge. While believers in Yeshua as the Messiah were being declared non-Jews, thousands of Lubavitch Hasidim were pronouncing their leader Menahem Schneerson the Messiah—and no one spoke of de-Jewing them. When some 400 Arab terrorists were deported to Lebanon, these three families facing deportation were not criminals or terrorists or enemies of the State, only lovers of Israel who wanted to live in the Land of their fathers. It seemed to us that God had prepared favor for our cause.

In January and February we held two press conferences; twenty-five reporters came to the one for the international media. As a result, articles appeared in the international edition of *Time* magazine, *The New York Times*, *The Chicago Tribune* and the various wire services. Cable News Network broadcast a 3-minute item to its 200,000,000 viewers. Israel television broadcast three public debates on the subject featuring the Beresfords, Joseph Shulam, and Gershon Nerel (the new Israel secretary of the International Messianic Jewish Alliance).

Meanwhile, the matter attracted the attention of a number of Knesset members, particularly those comprising the Human Rights Caucus. Three of these—Yossi Katz (Labor), Benni Temkin (Meretz) and Naomi Chazan (Meretz)—submitted a bill which would enable first-degree relatives (i.e. parents, children and spouses) of persons who had received the rights of a Jew under the Law of Return or who had served in the Israeli army to receive automatic permanent residence under the Law of Entry. As a result of their advocacy with the Ministry of the Interior, as well as a sizeable demonstration which we organized, the Kendalls and the Beresfords were granted visas to May 21, 1993 and the Speakmans to June 30.

A word about the demonstration and what led up to it. On February 11 we had a meeting at Beit Immanuel Congregation in Tel Aviv to explain to leaders throughout the Body the radically changed circumstances—by which I mean: no further hope in the courts, the need to rally behind these families for humanitarian and other reasons, a newly favorable publicity climate, friends in high political places, the willingness of us who had led and encouraged the court fights to admit error and sin. At a second meeting three days later a significant reconciliation took place between ourselves and some who had previously opposed us. We were able to unite on the idea of holding a demonstration against deporting the three families. An estimated 150–300 believers from throughout the country showed up February 21 in Jerusalem on a hill facing the Prime Minister's office. Present among the placards were reporters from newspapers, magazines, radio and television; the demonstration was seen on at least three Israel TV programs. I think it is no coincidence that it was also on this day that the Ministry of the Interior extended the visas. Smaller demonstrations continued for four more days.

Since then, those taking the long view organized themselves into The Committee for Three Messianic Jewish Families, of which I am Chairman, Shira Sorko-Ram Vice-Chairman, and Peter Tsukahira and Riki Drazni additional members of the "Bridging Committee", which discusses and guides activity. In March we decided to call for three days of prayer and fasting from Tuesday sundown to Friday sundown during the third complete week of each month from April to September. We have had three of these fasts, which have opened with prayer meetings on the Tuesday nights. The fasts have been publicized in newsletters, and we know that hundreds, perhaps thousands, of believers around the world have joined in these times of supplication before God. In addition, many have written letters requesting mercy in the matter from Interior Minister Aryeh Deri and Prime Minister Yitzchak Rabin; and other officials have been contacted. A number of Israeli non-Messianic Jews have sided publicly with our cause; particularly visible and active has been tour guide Micha Ashkenazi, whose every third sentence begins "I am not a believer, but..."

Meanwhile, there has been little outward activity since the

heady days of February. The Kendalls have left the Land for some rest and recuperation but are planning to return in July; we will be monitoring how they are dealt with and what kind of visas they get when they arrive. The Beresfords' visas expired; their request for new ones has been met with silence. Gary Beresford has flown out of Israel for the summer, and Shirley plans to follow in August; both intend to return in October, and we will be monitoring their return too. Sid Speakman has been researching his genealogy and has submitted the results to the Ministry of the Interior, which should have given an answer as of today (June 30) but has not. The Knesset bill is before the ministerial committee which decides whether the government coalition will back it (almost certainly crucial to its passage). Meanwhile, we fast and pray.

Also meanwhile, new facts are being created. Some Messianic Jews have made *aliyah.* Several have been turned back. The gentile spouse of a born Israeli Jew who has come to believe in Yeshua is apparently being denied olah status; we hope her application for permanent residence will be approved. Particularly disturbing to me was the Interior Ministry's refusal to grant amutah (charitable organization) status to the Messianic Jewish Alliance of Israel on the ground (explicitly, but in my view mistakenly, based on Beresford I) that the name misled the public into thinking that the organization was Jewish. The Interior Ministry was trying to apply the Law of Return definition of "Jew" to a different context entirely. As a board member of the MJAI I said it should fight for its rights in the court and not let the Ministry of Interior grab this new territory. But the board's decision was not to fight at this time and to apply again later.

Substantial expenses were incurred in all of this. The court imposed a fine of 15,000 shekels ($5,500). The three families have mostly had visas that did not permit them to earn a living in Israel, so their needs have had to be met. Lawyers, publicity activities and political campaigns require money. Persons interested in contributing, praying or receiving news may inquire through

Maos, Inc., Post Office Box 1414, Ramat HaSharon, Israel.

At present, we do not control the rhythm of events. The three families continue to hang there, sometimes with visas, sometimes without. The timing of events is determined by the Ministry of the Interior, Knesset committees and the media. If and when we bite the bullet and decide to campaign for a change in the Law of Return, we will be initiating events. Both ways of functioning have their place. The former is more relaxing, the latter more exciting!

We are aware that ultimately the battle is in the heavenlies. This is why we urge those who are with us to join us in our fasting and praying. Pray that the three families will get permanent residence, that no more Messianic Jews will be turned away, that the Law of Return will be changed to allow Messianic Jews to make *aliyah* openly and with heads held high, that unity will prevail in the Body of the Messiah in Israel, and that all Israel will be saved—speedily and in our days.